1 2 JUN 2019

Suffolk Libraries

Please return/renew this item
by the last date shown.

**Suffolk Libraries
01473 351249**
www.suffolklibraries.co.uk

By Dick Davis

POETRY

In the Distance 1975
Seeing the World 1980
The Covenant 1984
Lares 1986
Devices and Desires 1989
New and Selected Poems 1967–1987
A Kind of Love 1989
Selected and New Poems: USA
Touchwood 1996
Belonging 2002
A Trick of Sunlight 2007
At Home and Far from Home 2009
Poems on Iran and Persian Culture

VERSE TRANSLATIONS

Attar: The Conference of the Birds 1984
with Afkham Darbandi
Borrowed Ware 1996
Medieval Persian Epigrams
Ferdowsi: The Legend of Seyavesh 2004
Ferdowsi: Shahnameh 2006
The Persian Book of Kings
Gorgani: Vis and Ramin 2008
Faces of Love 2012
Hafez and the Poets of Shiraz
Fatemeh Shams: When They Broke Down the Door 2016

Dick Davis

Love in Another Language

COLLECTED POEMS
AND SELECTED TRANSLATIONS

CARCANET

First published in Great Britain in 2017 by

Carcanet Press Limited
Alliance House
Cross Street
Manchester M2 7AQ
www.carcanet.co.uk

We welcome your feedback: info@carcanet.co.uk

Copyright © Dick Davis 2017

The right of Dick Davis to be identified
as the author of this work has been asserted by him
in accordance with the Copyright, Designs
and Patents Act of 1988. All rights reserved.

A CIP catalogue record for this book is available
from the British Library, ISBN 978 1 78410 508 2

The publisher acknowledges financial assistance
from Arts Council England

Set in Monotype Bembo by Anvil
Printed and bound in England by SRP Ltd, Exeter

ACKNOWLEDGMENTS

Previously uncollected poems have appeared in *The Times Literary Supplement*, *The Hudson Review*, *New Criterion*, *The Hopkins Review*, *The Evansville Review*.

for Afkham

Contents

Prefatory Note   17

IN THE DISTANCE (1975)

The Diver	21
The Shore	22
Touring a Past	23
A Mycenaean Brooch	24
Scavenging After a Battle	25
Among Ruins	26
Byzantine Coin	26
The Expulsion from Eden	27
Diana and Actaeon	28
The Virgin Mary	29
St George and the Villagers	30
Childhood	31
Youth of Telemachus	31
Families	32
Reason in his Kingdom	33
Old Man Seated Before a Landscape	33
Service	34
Desire	34
Love in Another Language	35
Don Giovanni at the Opera	35
Irony and Love	36
The Epic Scholar	37
North-West Passage	38
Jesus on the Water	41
Ikon Angel	42
The Socratic Traveller	43
Anchorite	44
The Novice	44
Narcissus' Grove	44

Living in the World   45
Littoral   45
Reading After Opium   45
Buyer's Market   46
Names   46

SEEING THE WORLD (1980)

Travelling   49
Desert Stop at Noon   50
Night on the Long-Distance Coach   51
The City of Orange Trees   52
Syncretic and Sectarian   53
Memories of Cochin   53
Me, You   54
Marriage as a Problem of Universals   56
Don Giovanni   57
'Vague, vagrant lives . . .'   57
Government in Exile   58
Metaphor   58
Climbing   58
Dawn   59
Zuleikha Speaks   59
Simeon   61
St Christopher   62
Winter   62
Withernsea   63
A Recording of Giuseppe de Luca (1903)   64
False Light   64
Opening the Pyramid   65
Wittgenstein in Galway   65
An Entry   66
Philosopher and Metaphysics   66
Two Epigrams on Victory   67
Love   67
To Exorcize Regret   68
A Perfect Ending   68

Desire	69
Phaedra and Hippolytus	69
Rembrandt's *Return of the Prodigal Son*	70
Rembrandt Dying	70
Leonardo	72
On a Painting by Guardi	73
Epitaph	74
Maximilian Kolbe	74

THE COVENANT (1984)

Fräulein X	77
In the Gallery	78
Portrait Painter	78
What the Mind Wants	79
The Jigsaw	80
Annunciation	81
Four Visitations	
Baucis and Philemon	83
Semele	83
Jacob I	84
Jacob II	85
St Eustace	86
Getting There	87
'Uxor vivamus...'	87
To His Wife	89
Travelling	89
A Short History of Chess	90
Off-Shore Current	90
A Letter to Omar	91
Exiles	94
Woman on a Beach	95
Two East Anglian Poems	
With John Constable	96
Edward FitzGerald	96
The Tribe of Ben	97
A Photograph: Tehran, 1920s	98

Richard Davis	99
On an Etching by J. S. Cotman	100
Childhood of a Spy	101
Near Coltishall	102
The Ransom	103
Mariam Darbandi	104
Reading	105
My Daughter Sleeping	105
Auction – Job Lot	106
A Christmas Poem	107
Abandoned Churchyards	108
Hearing a Balkan Dance in England	108
Translating Hafez	109
Exile	110

LARES (1986)

Acedia	113
6 a.m. Thoughts	113
'And who is good? . . .'	114
Undine	114
Middle East 1950s	115
Ibn Battuta	116
The Departure of the Myths	117
Evening	118
Household Gods	119

DEVICES AND DESIRES (1989)

Jealousy	123
Wisdom	123
With Johnson's *Lives of the Poets*	124
Janet Lewis, Reading Her Poems	125
To the Muse	126
Magic	127
Making a Meal of It	128
The Sentimental Misanthrope	128

Made in Heaven	129
Heresy	129
Afkham	130

A KIND OF LOVE (1991)

Lady with a Theorbo	133
Qatran	134
Socrates' Daimon	134
Fatherhood	135
'Outside the snow…'	135
Three Versions of the Maker	136
Discipline	137
Learning a Language	137
Arghavan	138
Mohsen: A Gardener in California	138
On the Iranian Diaspora	140

TOUCHWOOD (1996)

To 'Eshqi	143
A Monorhyme for Miscegenation	146
Given Back, After Illness	147
After the Angels	148
Still	149
Your Children Growing	149
Comfort	150
Into Care	150
Pragmatic Therapy	151
Touchwood	151
Anthony 1946–1966	152
A Photograph of Two Brothers	152
The Suicide	153
Aftershocks	153
May	154
Going Home	154
A Sasanian Palace	155

Flight	156
Gold	157
Mirak	157
Names	159
We Should Be So Lucky	160
Masters	161
Tenured in the Humanities	161
New Reader	162
Art History	163
Epitaph	163
Couples	164
Old Couple	165
Middle Age	165
Repentance	166
Desire	166
A Tease	166
A Qasideh for Edgar Bowers on his Seventieth Birthday	167
In Praise of Auden	169
Suzanne Doyle's Poems	171
A Translator's Nightmare	172
Late	174
Fireflies	174

BELONGING (2002)

Shadows	177
A Monorhyme for the Shower	178
Haydn and Hokusai	179
Night Thoughts	180
Iran Twenty Years Ago	181
To the Persian Poets	182
Political Asylum	182
In History	183
Góngora	183
A Petrarchan Sonnet	184
Casanova	184

Dido	185
In the Restaurant	186
Duchy and Shinks	186
West South West	187
Teresia Sherley	188
What	191
'A world dies...'	191
'Sweet Pleasure...'	192
Hibernation	192
No Going Back	193
Secrets	194
Out of Time	194
Aubade	195
A Se Stesso	196
'Live happily'	197
Guides for the Soul	198
Games	199
Victorian	200
A Mind-Body Problem	202
Just a Small One, as You Insist	203
Desire	203
Farewell to the Mentors	204
A Bit of Paternity	205
Kipling's Kim, Thirty Years On	205
New at It	206
Déjà Lu	207
Growing Up	207
Old	208
Small Talk	208
At the Reception	208
Checking Out While Checking In	209
The Business Man's Special	209
Et in Arcadia Ego	209
Overheard in Khajuraho	209
Just So	210

A TRICK OF SUNLIGHT (2006)

'The heart has its abandoned mines...'	213
Chèvrefeuille	214
Getting Away	214
Water	216
Happiness	216
Hérédia	217
The Man from Provins	218
Before Sleep	219
The Old Model's Advice to the New Model	220
Edgar	221
Listening	222
What I Think	223
The Scholar as a Naughty Boy	224
Anglais Mort à Santa Barbara	224
The Sceptic	225
Driving	226
'Do you remember those few hours we spent'	226
Flying Back	227
Three Emilys	228
Turgeniev and Friends	229
Under $6 a Bottle	229
'They are not long, the days of wine and roses...'	230
Shopping	231
Chagrin	232
Pasts	232
A Visit to Grandmother's	233
Can We?	234
Cythère	235
Young Scholar	236
Farsighted	236
On a Remark of Karl Kraus	237
'I lay down in the darkness of my soul'	238
Preferences	238

Small Talk
   Not-Waking   239
   Imitatio   239
   'Live all you can; it's a mistake not to'   239
   Magic   239
   Soteriological   240
   'Interpretation is the revenge of the intellect upon art'   240
   Author, Translator...   240
   Damnation à la Mode   240
   Finding   240
   There   241
   Acculturation   241
   Spleen   241
The Phoenix   242
Dis's Defence   243
William McGonagall Welcomes the Initiative for a Greater Role for Faith-Based Education   244
William Morris   245
Driving Westward   246
Are We Going the Same Way?   247
Emblems   248
A Mystery Novel   248

NEW POEMS

A Storm in the Mid-West   251
The Lighthouse   251
A Personal Sonnet   252
To Take Courage in Childhood   253
Brahms   253
A Winter's Tale   254
The Missing Tale   255
Translating a Medieval Poem   255
Wil Mills (1969–2011)   256
Walking the Dog   257
The Fall   258
For my mother-in-law, during her last illness   259

A Dream	260
New Development	260
Darwinian	261
The Maple Tree	262
The Introduction	263
Wine	265
Admonition for the Seventh Decade	266
Campanilismo	266
Later	267
Keeping a Diary	268
Euro-trash	268
Paying for It	269
The Saving Grace	270
Going, going . . .	270
Reconnoitring	270
Leaving the Fair	271
To Vis	272
A Student Reading *Vis and Ramin*	272
Translating Hafez, or Trying To	273
WWHD?	274
Words	274

SELECTED TRANSLATIONS

Note on the Translations	277
From Farid ud-din Attar's *The Conference of the Birds*	
The Valley of Poverty and Nothingness	279
The Moths and the Flame	280
From *Borrowed Ware: Medieval Persian Epigrams*	282
From Ferdowsi's *Shahnameh: the Persian Book of Kings*	289
From Fakhraddin Gorgani's *Vis and Ramin*	292
From *Faces of Love: Hafez and the Poets of Shiraz*	
Poems by Hafez	305
Poems by Jahan Khatun	321

NOTES ON THE POEMS	339
INDEX OF TITLES	345

PREFATORY NOTE

The previously published poems included here are from six collections (*In the Distance*, 1975; *Seeing the World*, 1980; *The Covenant*, 1984; *Touchwood*, 1996; *Belonging*, 2002; *A Trick of Sunlight*, 2006), two retrospective volumes of Selected Poems (*Devices and Desires*, 1989; *A Kind of Love,* 1991), and a chapbook (*Lares*, 1986). The poems listed under *Devices and Desires* and *A Kind of Love* were new poems, at the time, included in these two volumes otherwise selected from previous books. The section entitled New Poems is made up of poems written since the publication of *A Trick of Sunlight* in 2006.

Like most habitual writers of poetry who live past middle age, I tend to prefer my more recent poems to the earlier ones – readers of course often disagree with poets' assessments of their own work – and for this reason I have omitted more poems from the earlier volumes than from the more recent ones. Although some of the earlier poems, including a number of those I've retained, now seem quite far from me in both their sensibility and the kinds of poems I was trying to make at the time, there is I think a discernible continuity of themes present from the earliest poems to the most recent; if I omitted all the poems to do with love, travel, the mixing of cultures, and the experience of being a stranger, this would be a very slim volume indeed.

I have been involved with Persian literature, particularly but not exclusively its medieval poetry, since I lived in Iran during the 1970s, and the closing section of this book features selections from my books of translations from medieval Persian poetry. My fascination with the great poets of medieval Iran has only deepened and broadened over the years, and I could not imagine a Collected Poems that did not include some indication of this by now essential part of my life.

DICK DAVIS

In the Distance

THE DIVER

for Michaelis Nicoletséas

The blue-cold spasm passes,
And he's broken in.
Assailed by silence he descends
Lost suddenly

To air and sunburned friends,
And wholly underwater now
He plies his strength against
The element that

Slows all probings to their feint.
Still down, till losing
Light he drifts to the wealthy wreck
And its shade-mariners

Who flit about a fractured deck
That holds old purposes
In darkness. He hesitates, then
Wreathes his body in.

THE SHORE

He feels against his skin
Throughout the night the pulse
Of her unchanging sleep:
Delicately, within
Her grasp and warmth, he rolls
Aside to watch the deep

Thought may not sound: her face
And body are a blur
Of breathing shadow, where,
Beyond that gentle pace,
He may by love infer
The darkness of her hair,

Her covered eyes, the shape
Of hands still touching his,
Her mouth: but nothing more.
If he, by stealth or rape,
Would seize her mind he is
Held helpless at the shore –

Impatient, lost: she goes
Untraced beyond the gleams
Of intellect, control –
He waits, but never knows
What demons or what dreams
Possess her voyaging soul.

TOURING A PAST

The ruins, which are not very remarkable, are situated on an island which is almost impossible to reach . . .
Hachette Guide to the Middle East, p. 1003

Even from here I see
How stagnant and unused
The brackish waters lie,
As if the bank had oozed
This stream that sluggishly
Reflects the idle sky.

There is no boat to cross
From that ill-favoured shore
To where the clashing reeds
Complete the work of war
Together with the grass,
And nesting birds, and weeds.

I read that now there is
Almost no evidence –
No walls or pottery –
Of what I know were once
The walks and palaces
Love lent to you and me.

A MYCENAEAN BROOCH

> ... *and we*
> *Shall set our feet in peace on lesser isles.*
> YVOR WINTERS

Peace came back slowly, sealed
In iron, to which there
Is no answer. Wounds healed,

But silence guards Mycenae
Where I beat out useless
Bronze to fend off history.

From our last swords broken
Blades I made my wife this
Brooch, survivor's token

Of her fathers' armour –
Though bronze will not protect
And may endanger her.

We shall leave for Ionia:
There islands may exist,
Too small for them, or far.

SCAVENGING AFTER A BATTLE

Cold rimed on the metal,
The slam of the sea on the gravel –

Stone warriors and overturned horses,
He picks his way among corpses.

Diligently he
Severs gold, hacks the stones free

Of their rusting heraldic moulds –
Rubies; sapphires; emeralds.

Colour cupped in his hand; the sea
And the clouds cold grey.

AMONG RUINS

Rest here and fantasize the willing past
That like a lover answers to your mood:
You know her kind deceptions will not last
(And even now they only half delude).

But as nude bodies meet with stolen pride
And in their lust renounce all mental ills –
Leaving sad individual lives outside
The locked room where the animal fulfils

Himself, herself – so in this bright ruin
Sweet history shall tease and beckon you,
And as she moves seem free of ancient sin,
Half-lit, and only partially untrue.

BYZANTINE COIN

How many hands, vicissitudes,
Have worn this gold to the thin ghost
That gleams in the shopkeeper's palm?
A millennium flickers, eludes
Us, is gone, as we bend engrossed
In blurred words and a surface charm.

THE EXPULSION FROM EDEN

The broad sword goads them and the flame
Drives onward to the gate of shame

That clangs behind them as a curse.
Cast out they pause, confused.
                              What was

The meaning of that naked place –
What is the vague cold world they face
Immeasurably random here?
Their slow hands link in silent fear
As to each indistinct horizon
Extend blank vistas of confusion
Where they must go, unsheltered, free,
And by acquired hostility
Wrest sustenance and weak defence
From chaos and indifference.

Distraught affection holds them close
Who have no knowledge but their loss –

They move: their unsure feet descend
To worlds they cannot comprehend.

DIANA AND ACTAEON

He strays from sun to shade
And hears his favourite hound
Cry in some distant glade
That the tired deer is bayed.

At once, almost, the sound
Cannot be placed: he peers
Distractedly around
At unfamiliar ground.

The vagueness that he hears,
The eucalyptus trails,
Chafe at his nascent fears –
This way and that he veers,

Trapped, simple flesh: details
Half-lost between the trees
Cohere, and reason fails.
The goddess stoops, unveils –

Then naked stands, at ease,
Laved by the swirling stream:
Her hair stirs on the breeze,
And as he stares he sees

Her eyes fix his. They gleam
With infinite disdain.
His dogs' jaws snarl, but seem
Elsewhere – till through the dream

He feels the gash of pain.

THE VIRGIN MARY

All these oppressed her:
                    light's
Peremptory pure glare
In summer, and the weak
Pallor of winter air;
Men's breath against her cheek,
And fruitless unshared nights.

Her strange clothes hung in mute
Annoying folds. She dreamed
Of splendour, undefined.
Naked, her body seemed
The useless withered rind
Of some prodigious fruit . . .

As if a distant call
Abstracted her, she bore
Her days indifferently,
And waited vaguely for
One slight contingency
That would resolve them all.

ST GEORGE AND THE VILLAGERS

for Clive Wilmer

He laughed to see his life
Thus simplified, the quest
Completed and the rife
Contingencies at rest.

The unequivocal
Entirely evil beast
Reared at his brazen call:
Now sure that at the least

His purpose was not base
Or trivial he smote
With an abandoned grace
The massive coiling throat.

The villagers, the evil
Of whose lives was never
Pure nor whole nor simple,
Watched their deliverer –

Aware that other beasts
Would come, when he had gone
To princesses and feasts
Believing he had won.

CHILDHOOD

for Robert Wells

Imperceptible, at sunrise, the slight
Breeze stirs the dreaming boy, till silently
He edges free from sleep and takes the kite,
Huge on his shoulders like an angel's wings,
To climb the hill beyond the drowsing city.
Released, the first ungainly waverings

Are guided out, above the still valley,
Constrained to one smooth flow, diminishing
Until the pacing boy can hardly see
The dark dot shift against the constant blue:
He squats and stares: in his hand the taut string
Tugs, strains – as if there were still more to do.

YOUTH OF TELEMACHUS

It is a land he knows. White sunlight
Specifies each shrub and stone –
And as he moves his vacant sight
Restores him to the ways he's grown:

He is enclosed in reveries
No will can break, and where he goes
A child's unfinished fantasies
Dictate the paths that he will choose.

He rises in the dawn: the sun
Illuminates where he will pause
And where proceed: at his return
He sleeps and dreams his father's wars:

Until one evening he delays,
Past sunset, sunk in memory:
He sees the moon rise and he stays:
All night he views the changing sea.

FAMILIES

Confronted with the attic
He realized he could never clear
The clutter gathered there.

The photographs' recesses
Told him to depart,
The faces mocked his heart

That humbly would be kind
Too late. They would not allow
His hand to tear them now.

He could not efface them,
Things denied since death,
Nor would they be his myth.

Neither gone nor holy
They heard impassively
His childish . . . 'sorry'.

REASON IN HIS KINGDOM

Sad, errant Reason, having no weapons, wandered
In the world's wood that someone had once said
Was his to rule. He knew it had been squandered
Among others, and disinherited
His shadow traced the things it did not own.
The fences and the crisp consoling view
Were cluttered with tough weeds and overgrown
With tangled thorns. He watched. What could he do

Who heard the bitter cries and saw the blood
Dry slowly at the roots of trees where life
Confused and blind fought vilely through the mud
Of other lives? Sad Reason gazed on strife
And recognized his impotence: his stare
Grew imprecise with inwardness, despair.

OLD MAN SEATED BEFORE A LANDSCAPE

generations, as the wind-blown leaves . . .

In a strengthless wind the near leaves falter:
They are cold: frost will decide their posture.

To watch unsettles him: each separate
Discrete particular, an animate

Uncertain will claiming attention: no.
The distant unclimbed hills dissolve and glow

With evening light: the vague unfocused mass
In which particulars of rock and grass

Are lost and merged in indistinct coherence
Restores vague peace, and his awareness loosens

Toward sleep: his book slips: loose pages flutter
In the cold wind. He had been reading Homer.

SERVICE

Mismanaged love, at large, made vagrant,
Uncontained seeking the enormous land

Seen fleetingly, once manifest, now lost:
Seeking the defining rite, the service

That the heart could bend to – of rosary,
Or gun, or patient domesticity.

DESIRE

Dry summer heat:
Dark roses glimmer from the plane tree's shade –

Parched love: O face
That lives, a dull obsession in the mind.

LOVE IN ANOTHER LANGUAGE

A stream irregularly dammed
    With unshaped stones
That swerve the current in its course –

    The meaning crammed
Through unfamiliar channels, in new tones,
    With a choked force.

DON GIOVANNI AT THE OPERA

God is not here nor there, though there
    Breasts swell to the attack
Of Mozart, and her loose dark hair
    Spills on her naked back.

God is not here nor there, though there
    The new soprano sings
Betrayed Elvira's wild despair,
    Plucking his nerves like strings.

God is not here nor there, though there,
    In the interval, gin
Glitters, winks, and the dark girl's stare
    Is answered with a grin.

God is not here nor there, though there
    Sensation eases thought:
The whispers of a new affair
    Beguile, and he is caught.

IRONY AND LOVE

Irony does not save:
The knowledge that you repeat
The infantile indiscreet
Reactions of the dead

Does not save. Irony
Says nothing when her hand
Gestures the promised land.
Irony is the dead

Who are not saved but see
Magnificent bold Orpheus
Claim the incredulous
Soon-to-return Eurydice.

THE EPIC SCHOLAR

What is his life? the library,
    Worn books minutely scanned,
The evening and the single meal.
    He dreams of the vast land.

He sees behind the urtext loom
    The dedicated band
Who, barbarous, inhabit him:
    He dreams of the vast land.

A scholar's indolence: the shelves
    Dissolve to endless sand;
Horizons touched, lost enmities:
    He dreams of the vast land.

His patience thins: minutiae:
    His predecessors planned
The complex text impeccably:
    He dreams of the vast land,

His solitary action there:
    O he can understand
His love's futility: but look,
    He dreams of the vast land.

NORTH-WEST PASSAGE

To seek new worlds for gold, for praise, for glory
SIR WALTER RALEIGH

The green sea lapped, a liquid jade.
That too was theirs, or soon. They saw
The drenched green dream of England fade

And fracture in the sluice and pour
Of Arctic waves. Their villages
Bobbed quietly, and were no more:

Small jagged ice-floes took their place
And nudged and clustered round the ship
As if they followed, keeping pace

With its unsteady yaw and slip.
Low cloud obscured the sky, and snow
Began to fall, and like a whip

Brine-soaked they felt the cold spray blow
Against their cracked unhardened skin.
They saw the raw wounds split and grow.

Ice glistened in the rigging, thin
And spectral as the silver veins
Threading the ore that they would win.

North-west: illimitable gains
Shone vaguely through the frozen mist
And they assuaged their bodies' pains

With hope, numb promises. North-west:
But slower now; beneath the weight
Of ice the ship would dip and list

As if the yards were animate
And leant in thwarted amity
Toward their final, restless, fate.

Men, silent, watched the ice-clogged sea
And felt their small ship shudder, strain,
And slow, and slow, perceptibly:

And in the night the livid stain
Of ice against the dark rose high
Above the watch, who saw disdain,

Malevolence, and in his cry
Of 'Ice-bergs! Ice-bergs!' heard that fear
He had suppressed, that he would die.

But ceaselessly, beneath the sheer
Harsh cliffs of ice, the helmsman's hand
Lay motionless, as if to steer

North-west through all his life. Low land
Appeared, an inhospitable
And lifeless waste, to port, ice-bound:

The sea became invisible
Beneath the sliding ice that scraped
The ship in rhythm to the swell,

Until the slowed hull trembled, stopped,
Stuck firm between the massive floes,
At last, irrevocably, gripped.

Their nights grew longer, and the snows
That swirled about the stranded hulk
Disguised the distant shore-line, froze

Their food, their friendship, boredom, talk;
Their limbs, their minds. Indifferently
They heard the timbers crack, the bulk-

Heads buckle, gape; for they could see
Slow scurvy undermine their friends
Insidiously and totally

As ice that saps and weakens, bends
And snaps their rotting ship. Their food
Exhausted, stubborn hunger sends

Them hunting, but no hopes delude
Their lonely search. As they return
Across the hard-packed ice they brood

On human flesh, and one by one
The lots are cast. They kill, they die –
And though the lots are cast again,

Again, uneaten bodies lie
Preserved till spring, then lapped and rolled
By waves beneath the Arctic sky;

And waves disperse their dreams of gold
Who had not thought the world could be
So small, so comfortless, so cold.

JESUS ON THE WATER

Walking through this
Specious evening I've
Become at last aware
That no specific
Can contain my stare.

And this gaze my father
Gave is imaged in this
Stride, this hunger
To be past such
Syllables of rumour –

So one stone would jar
My steps, and I could cry
Just once, 'Just here'.
But my feet tread water
Only, as a stare

That blurs particulars
In tears. So intangibly
I wander, envy Peter
Rock and weight, and
All his sea-drenched hair.

IKON ANGEL

The half-coiled loop of his body
And the scarlet drape of his cloak
Slipping from the moulded breastplate
Hardly reveal his lax, slim weight
Against the spear, as if he slept,
Ignorant of the family

Whose human and hieratic Child
Leans with new-born solemnity
To bless the kneeling worshipper.
But the Angel, God's warrior,
Is vigilant beyond this place –
He gazes, blank, unreconciled:

What is this mock humanity –
This sweet charade of mother, child,
Kind animals and gorgeous kings,
This bric-à-brac of trivial things
That reassure the simplest faith –
To him, who sees eternity?

THE SOCRATIC TRAVELLER

Beneath the inconsistent skies
He moves, in sun and sudden rain,
The rinsed air following, his eyes
Undaunted, as if unaware
Of what might turn aside their stare
And mitigate the real terrain.

He begs the truth of all he sees –
The city and the village, plain
And moorland stream, the crowded trees,
Each street, each desolate high hill –
He finds no meaning but he will
Not mitigate the real terrain:

He prosecutes his pilgrimage
Toward the sceptic's partial gain
Of seeing what is false – the gauge
Of truth becomes whatever he
Cannot discern as sophistry
That mitigates the real terrain.

Until he penetrates by slow
Degrees to ignorance, the vain
Obverse of all that he would know:
And, pausing, he is made aware
It is his constant presence there
That mitigates the real terrain.

ANCHORITE

He moves, in the debilitating heat,
Flesh wormed and riddled as an ikon's gold,
Light-headed from the lack of food, toward
The soul's oasis, an incorporal shade.

THE NOVICE

An exiled Oedipus, he makes his way
Through the stunned crowd, sentenced by his own code:

Such sex and power were his, and what were they?
Sightless he stumbles toward the open road.

NARCISSUS' GROVE

A place for the evasive, self-lockt stare,
The useless beauty that the world disowns:

Water sedulous over the grey stones –
The pines' sweet resin scents the sleeping air.

LIVING IN THE WORLD

Abandoned dreams, of sainthood or rusticity,
The pure heroics that the child desired,
Disturb the sleeper, lapsed in promiscuity –
His will dispersed, and unappeased, and tired.

LITTORAL

Salt smoothes and sand obliterates
The trite, the once-dear vestiges

Mute hieroglyphs, the hulks of pomp
And sea-worn amulets of love.

READING AFTER OPIUM

Precise and indefinable: like scent
The drug diffuses, eddies, in his mind.

'God', 'love':
          he gropes to what the words once meant,
As if these gentle pastures had been mined.

BUYER'S MARKET

Whether you glitter in Athens or Florence
There is always, at last, grandiloquent Rome –
Waiting to formalize insights and talents
And making your patron completely at home.

NAMES

Inapprehensible, the world: what was,
Once, almost palpable, is now become
The names of absences: tree, face, water.

I journey toward another absence, one
I dare not name, but whisper as I place
My steps, like a child's skipping-rhyme, 'Lord, Lord'.

Seeing the World

TRAVELLING

1   *Pastoral*

Wild lavender and mint;
                     the mind's bemused
Sheep browse – cropping the serious anecdote,
Eschewing the dust of small-talk.
                            Nearby,

Reason is a small boy who throws stones, sends
His yapping dog, to guide the errant flock.

2   *An Arrival*

Stranger, accept the little that is given –
The evening crowds, the quick unlooked-for smile
And the benediction of the sunset:
                              who knows
But the tryst with the unknown god is here?

DESERT STOP AT NOON

    The house is one bare room
    And only tea is served.
    The old man, mild, reserved,
    Shuffles into a gloom
    Where mattresses are laid.
I sip, grateful for the cool shade.

    His small son watches me,
    Approaches, pertly smiles.
    I know that thirty miles
    Without a house or tree
    Surround their crumbling shack.
I drink again, relax, smile back.

    Water? and the boy's mother?
    Both seem impossible –
    Yet, here, my glass is full;
    If I ask for another
    The boy brings bitter tea
Then grins gap-toothed and begs from me.

    And love? Impertinence
    To ask. I could not grieve,
    Born here, to have to leave:
    But he, a man, years hence,
    His life elsewhere, may weep
With need to see his father sleep

    Again, as now he does,
    In careless honesty –
    Too old for courtesy –
    Oblivious of us.
    I pay, and leave the shade,
The dark recess these lives have made.

NIGHT ON THE LONG-DISTANCE COACH

At last it is too dark to read.
I stare out on indifference,
A moonlit world that does not need
Our charity or deference.

And there my unfleshed face stares back,
Thin ghost through which far mountains show,
A palimpsest whose features lack
The constancy that lies below.

Below lie rock and scrub, the plain
Whence rodent eyes peer into mine –
An instant of inhuman pain
Deranges all I would define –

And I, and those I journey to,
Seem shadows without consequence,
A ghostly bustling to and fro
Through wastes of lunar permanence.

THE CITY OF ORANGE TREES

'The city filled with orange trees
Is lost', which, interpreted, meant
All conspicuous luxuries
Augur ruinous punishment.

This fitted what he knew. The zeal
For conquest, prayer, decays; the child
Mocks pieties he cannot feel
And children's children are beguiled

By comfort, gardens, literature.
Aesthetics dazes them, safe lives
Grow lax and soon they can endure
No one but slaves, musicians, wives . . .

Till to degeneracy the Lord
Sends one who, like their forbears, spurns
Mere taste as mannered cant. The sword
Falls and the plundered city burns.

        ★   ★   ★

Heir to three generations' learning,
He closed his book, his masterpiece.
Silk rustled as he rose, turning,
Ready to parley now for peace

With one beyond the city gate
Who, barbarous, impatient, vain,
No vows or presents could placate –
The world-conqueror, Tamburlaine.

SYNCRETIC AND SECTARIAN

If, unbeguiled by that suspicious wraith
Called Purity, we look with favour on
    The nebulous, syncretic faith
Of Shah Jahan's first-born, unworldly son –

(Translating Hindu scriptures into Persian,
Convinced the sadhu and the sufi were
    Lost brothers squabbling for the version
Of one tremendous truth) we must refer,

As well, to that blunt, younger brother who
– Contemptuous of vapid heresy –
    Was more than eager to pursue
(By fratricide) the wraith of Purity.

MEMORIES OF COCHIN

An epithalamium

Through high defiles of warehouses that dwarf
With undetermined age the passer-by,
    We walk toward the ancient wharf
Assailed by smells – sweet, pungent, bitter, dry:

The perfumed plunder of a continent.
To this shore Roman, Moslem, Christian, Jew
    Were gathered by the dense, sharp scent;
Absorbed now in the once-outlandish view

They camped by hills their children would call home.
So in the soil blurred Roman coins are found;
      Saint Thomas stepped into the foam
And strode ashore, and blessed the acrid ground;

Jews settled here when Sion was laid waste,
And Arabs edged tall dhows into the bay,
      Dutch burghers felt their northern haste,
Becalmed by slow siestas, ebb away...

So many faiths and peoples mingle here,
Breathing an air benign with spice and scent,
      That we, though strangers, should not fear
To invoke, in honour of our sacrament,

The sensual, wise genius of this place.
Approach, kind god: bestow your gifts on two,
      Your votaries, of different race
Made one, by love, by marriage, and by you.

ME, YOU

I am deceived
At first, but no —
You are asleep.
As if you grieved
For some lost glow
Of love, your deep

Dream moves your hand
To seek my skin
And there discover
The well-known land:
Somewhere within
Your brain a lover

Leaves you and you
Reach out to hold
Him close. I touch
Your body too –
As if he told
You what you clutch

Toward, your sleep
Grows still – and now
My hand explores
The silent deep
Of breast and brow.
My hand withdraws.

Now sleep is ours,
Quiet, till dawn
Will wake us to
The separate hours
And we are torn
Apart – me, you.

MARRIAGE AS A PROBLEM OF UNIVERSALS

for Meera and Navin Govil

    Marriage is where
The large abstractions we profess
Are put gently in their small place –
    The holist's stare
In love with Man has managed less
Than eyes that love one ageing face.

    Marriage believes
The universals we desire
Are children of a worldly care –
    While Plato grieves
For stasis, the refining fire
Men pass through is the lives they share.

    Marriages move
Between the symbol and life's facts,
From Beauty to this troubled face –
    Though what we love
Is Truth, Truth flares and fades in acts
Of local, unrecorded grace.

DON GIOVANNI

The unkissed mouth, unsubjugated eyes
Flower in the vacant air...
                              slashed down they rise

In mocking, gossipy, distracting swarms,
A ghastly hydra of unconquered forms...

He rides forward. Poor knight, poor travesty –
His quest uncertain, his adversary
At once monotonous and protean,
His loneliness immense, his armour gone
Except the shield,
                      which bears this sad device
'I know that something somewhere will suffice'.

'VAGUE, VAGRANT LIVES...'

Vague, vagrant lives, elusive, almost,
As the vision that they seek, at home
Nowhere...
                      they pause before each landscape
With impartial eyes, as if they stood
Here only to collate, compare, then
Move again, assured...
                        drawn still nearer
To an understanding not yet found.

GOVERNMENT IN EXILE

Silence, and on the wall the photographs —
Farms, mountains, faces; the sad specifics
Corrode the heart, sharpen the will. Despair
Is shrugged away and stares one in the face.

Loyalty is poured out — a libation
To childhood villages, to stones, to trees.

METAPHOR

Emotion flares, and is absorbed: almost
At peace you watch the opalescent west.
Light fades: a flock of birds starts up and wheels
And scatters in the sky, and recombines,
And settles as the first stars shine, intense
As loss, small points of agony, sharp signs
That glitter in the sky's immense grey waste.

CLIMBING

Enter the clarity you love —
The high thin air above the clouds
That in the wintry wind disperse

Like a mind clearing, like the fading
Of a loved illusion
                so that you see
The world with unencumbered eyes.

Here, at the summit, at your feet,
Stretches the black volcanic pool,
The dark Avernus of the self.

DAWN

You cannot say what sense it is through which
You understand but it is like the wind
That gently chill-ly tugs the desert plants
And leaves them undisturbed or like the air
That preternaturally reveals the hills
Or like the silence through which nothing sounds
Like words. Light spreads and speaks. You understand
It is that truth you need not understand.

ZULEIKHA SPEAKS

Gentle, then cruel — the same
Half-masked indifference
Dulls both. I say your name,
'Husband'. With what loathed sense

Am I yours, you mine? Night
Gives me to you but I
Shrink from its shameful rite,
Your energy and sigh,

The weight you think I love:
And in the day you watch,
Laugh, grumble, bargain – move
Beyond my woman's touch.

Now though you are not here.
I see the goats brought in,
The gilded dust, and hear
The world's unfocused din –

(Kids' startled hooves, boys' cries,
Somewhere a flute). The dim
Gold twilight weakens, dies.
I stay. I think of him,

The stranger –
             as reticent,
Ineffable, as is
This sun's unprized descent.
I know that I am his.

The cold wind stirs my dress.
The desert stars appear.
My husband calls. I bless
His name, but shall not hear.

SIMEON

Luke II.26

How long now since
The vow was made...
Yet still he haunts
The temple's shade

Silent to those
Who say he dreamed
The angelic face.
Its splendour gleamed

More harshly than
The sacral knife
Caught by the sun,
And seared his life

To a blank daze
Of memory...
The half-glimpsed face
Of certainty.

As if that pause
When Abraham
Through lawless tears
Beheld the ram

Had been delayed
For centuries,
The falling blade
As on a frieze.

ST CHRISTOPHER

Curled fingers tighten in his curly hair:
But if, by any prescience, he knows
The nature of that burden He must bear
Whom now he bears, no recognition shows.

The weathered body and tenacious mind
Venture like partners with but one intent –
Lo, they are one, as cautiously they find
The safe stones through the unsafe element.

And thus, subsumed by what he does, made sure
That though his task is humble it is good,
He navigates toward the further shore –
Secure in skill and patient hardihood.

WINTER

Your moment comes, inapprehensible.
Autumnal cold pervades the mountain pool;
The tense, still surface glistens; it is ice.
I peer, but cannot see what lives or dies.

Quotidian despair, I feel your cold lips
Searching me in the dark, your soft hand grips
With an enormous strength: I tremble, yours.
It is your hand that guides me now, explores

The vacant world for me.
                      I walk at night,
Possessed by the cold: on a building-site
Smoke from the watchman's fire smarts in my eyes:
Brief greetings clash, like gravel thrown on ice.

WITHERNSEA

Stones, sand, I have not seen in fourteen years;
A place for childhood's self-communing tears,

For wandering. I walked the moonlit beach
An adolescent whom no waves could teach

The simplest truth of life, that nothing lasts:
I scavenged among poetries and pasts

For something glittering, precise and sure.
In winter-storms gigantic breakers tore

The cliff's vermilion mud into the sea.
The weakening edge seeps vaguely, constantly.

A RECORDING OF GIUSEPPE DE LUCA (1903)

The record's hiss — so dense
You hardly hope to hear
The voice rise sweet and clear
Beyond its violence —

Seems like the sea-wash of
Time's old opacity
As it indifferently
Obscures the things we love.

But with what poignant strength
The voice soars free of time —
The young man in his prime
Still careless of the length

Of laggard years ahead,
Of that attrition which
No beauty can bewitch...
The youth so long now dead.

FALSE LIGHT

See where the landscape glows and flares
Lit by the beacons of desire —

As faces grouped about a fire
Give back the light that is not theirs.

OPENING THE PYRAMID

Though you recall the emphatic starlight
When the angels said, 'Follow, we shall lead',

Irony, like the free air and sunlight,
Crumbles the mummy of each simple creed.

WITTGENSTEIN IN GALWAY

O come unto these yellow sands
Alone.
       The slow work of his hands,

Secluded by sad policy,
His hut opposed the breaking sea

Whose meaningless unchanged refrain
Might one day still the circling brain.

★   ★   ★

Things that could never be thought of
Were metaphysics, anguish, love.

And though his tamed gulls swooped for bread
He lived, like us, inside his head

Locked out of that vast privacy
Of stones and sand, wild gulls and sea.

AN ENTRY

When one is frightened of the truth (as I am now) then it is never the whole truth that one has an inkling of.
WITTGENSTEIN: *Notebooks*, 15.10.1914

To what strange sum could you be reconciled
That could atone for consciousness adrift
In grandeur it can never comprehend,

For suffering, for death?
                              What glimpse beguiled
You of our fear? What hand disclosed what gift
In token that blind passion has an end?

PHILOSOPHER AND METAPHYSICS

If shocked outsiders sympathize
With his neglected, brilliant wife

They have been spared the specious lies,
The skittish charm that wrecked his life.

TWO EPIGRAMS ON VICTORY

1

Wotan and Prospero
Grown wise in tribulation know
   Whose is the victory,
And envy his simplicity.

2

Life narrows to the things you did not mean;
The endless vista is a painted screen.

Now, like the Count in *Figaro*, you see
Forgiveness where you ogled victory.

LOVE

Later her heart will blur with pain

(He sleeps. Her hand strays in his hair,
Impulsive, indolent.
                She says,
'I love you' to the morning air.)

Now the years say nothing to her.

TO EXORCIZE REGRET

Grant the patience to accept
What the heart would still reject

May the distance be mere space
Grant the grace to need no grace

May flesh be flesh —
                         never again
Source and symbol of such pain.

A PERFECT ENDING

    These two now meet
Under no god's tutelage —
    Their smiles, discreet,
Need no reserves of courage:

    These two, who once
Were adepts, are polite —
    These celebrants
Agree to smooth the rite

    To an aesthete's
Memory: renouncing Eros
    Their brisk chat treats
As 'youth' once-frantic loss.

DESIRE

Of the violence of that pain
What poor traces still remain —

This I learnt: the wry technique
Of avoiding what I seek.

PHAEDRA AND HIPPOLYTUS

She felt the virgin's tentative
Thin lips brush stiff against her own —

Reluctant flesh, that would disown
Mere human need, that could not live.

REMBRANDT'S *RETURN OF THE PRODIGAL SON*

Age instinct with wisdom, love, bends towards
The sensual man, the penitent, and clasps
Him lightly by the shoulder-blades. In rags
The latter kneels and rests his close-cropped head
Against the Father's chest. Some watch, and one,
Whose face is lit, old as the Father, looks
With unobserved compassion at the scene.

His comprehension is the artist's own:
His silence and the Father's flood the frame
But cannot quite subdue the young man's sobs,
The fixed, sad past; the waste that love would heal.

REMBRANDT DYING

    What have I known?
    The darkness I perceived
Beyond each face invades my mind,
    I have been shown
    The night of the bereaved
In which all men are blind.

    But I recall
    Old faces marred, their eyes
Outstaring that obscurity –
    Awaiting all
    Life yet may ask with wise,
Unbroken, dignity;

  And the young Jew
  Who was my Christ, in whose
As-if-omniscient, worn face
  Compassion grew –
  Where patience could peruse
  The sufferings of a race;

  And Hendrickje
  Who taught me tenderness,
So that the proof of all technique
  Was to convey
  Love's truths – light on a dress,
  Or on her turning cheek.

  All these are past –
  The darkness wells in me;
Though grief and ignorance increase
  And must outlast
  My will, yet memory
  Is thankful for lost peace.

LEONARDO

whose Last Supper *began to break up in his own life-time*

My years were given
To permanence –
The arrested dance,
Emblem of heaven.

Decay invades
The icon of
Eternal love:
My emblem fades

Like human skin:
The wrinkles grow
As if paint too
Partook of sin.

Late, late I see
The meaning of
Incarnate love,
Eternity.

ON A PAINTING BY GUARDI

    Slowly the chill lagoon
Returns to flood these noisome ponds;
    Grotesque, dense weeds festoon
The ruined arch with airy fronds

    In whose shade scavengers
– Tenacious as the trailing weeds –
    Time's ghostly avatars,
Indifferent to the grace that feeds

    Their chance cupidity,
Draw strength from glory in decay.
    Great Mutability,
All here declares your mordant sway.

    I gaze, hardly aware
Of this overt, didactic aim:
    Rather the misty air,
The blank, amorphous shore proclaim

    An eye in love with blurred
And insubstantial forms, a mind
    By evanescence stirred –
A suppliant of the undefined,

    The pale marsh-haze of noon;
And one who in each breeze could see
    – Ruffling the chill lagoon –
The tremor of mortality.

EPITAPH

I betrayed and I was betrayed.
Wistful for righteousness I added to
  The world's evil. Invoke my shade
With gentleness; this grief will be yours too.

MAXIMILIAN KOLBE

O crux ave spes unica

Secure, afraid, I contemplate
The fearless necessary fate
Of one who, undisturbed by crime,
Became himself his Paradigm.

The Covenant

FRÄULEIN X

*And it turned out that with her thanks for the poison
Fräulein X had still one more request: would the friend
sing Brahms's 'Vier ernste Gesänge' before they parted.*

DIARY OF RECK-MALLECZEWEN, December 1938

Unseen, preserved beneath dark velvet, lie
Pale water-colours fugitive to light –
Displayed to none but friendship's gentler eye,
The sanctuaries of her sequestered sight –

Views of the Rhine and of the Holy Land,
Deep vistas of the spirit's need and rest:
Frail on glass shelves Venetian glasses stand,
The keepsakes of a life secure and blessed.

Now, in this last desire, she redeclares
Old faith in what is hers – Judaic psalms,
The German tongue: that heritage she shares
– Immutably – with Luther and with Brahms:

And though that sheltered world her childhood knew
Is shrunk to a dark room, though in the street
The mob bays hatred to the German Jew,
This covenant survives, beyond defeat.

IN THE GALLERY

O patria mia!

One drawing held her; it was of
An indistinct but Eastern view
And had no special charm: her hand
Strayed to the glass as if she knew
The contours of that barren land
And could not stare at them enough:

I saw her beauty then, the love
Made steady in her exiled eyes:
Those lines were faint as memory,
Effaced as the elusive sighs
That scarcely broke her revery;
I watched, withheld, and could not move.

PORTRAIT PAINTER

If, in the middle-aged
Worn face now given to
His stranger's scrutiny
He sees – unbidden, true –
Regret stare unassuaged
From posed formality –

Her need and loss, a life
Of compromise made plain,
His thoughts are not the rush

Of sympathy for pain
But tone and palette-knife,
The texture of this brush:

And, glancing up, his gaze
Meets nothing of the heart
But colour, shade, and gloss –
The problems of his art;
While from the canvas blaze
Discovered need and loss.

WHAT THE MIND WANTS

Young aspens mirrored in a stream;
A guileless evanescence, an
Unguided turning to the wind.

But also the persistent weight
Of glassy water, the steady
Pressure that seems barely moving;

The windless, slow, reflective depth.

THE JIGSAW

for Sarah Davis

The portrait of the princess lies
In scattered fragments on the floor;
Crouched over them a young girl tries
Edges that would not fit before,

That sulk recalcitrant . . . ah there
Two pieces kiss: a greyish mass
That could be clouds or that patch where
Her dress half hides the shadowed grass.

The afternoon wears on: she sifts
And sorts; a piece is placed, withdrawn;
She sits up suddenly and lifts
Impatient arms. A stifled yawn.

And stoops again. Here no one wins,
It is a world you make and enter.
The edge is finished – now begins
The serious business of the centre.

A face emerges and young hands
Lie loose against grey silk; the eyes
Are guileless: almost there, she stands
Bent slightly forward in surprise.

ANNUNCIATION

Thin-shouldered, shy,
And much alone –
Anxious to screen
The monotone

Of her young life
From avid eyes,
The curious gaze
Disarmed by sighs,

By silence ... but,
At heart, ashamed –
As if she knew
That she were blamed

For some dark sin
Unspecified –
As if the flesh
That broke her pride

Were penance for
An obscure fault
Not to be cleansed
In her tears' salt.

★

The morning lightens
Through poplar trees –
Her flushed skin takes
Dawn's sober breeze

As promise of
The known and real
To which she would
But cannot kneel.

And the light deepens
Beyond the line
Of glittering trees;
Their thin leaves shine

Till they are lost
In whelming light
Like water breaking . . .
She shields her sight

And hears the words
That justify
Her flesh, her life . . .
The unearthly cry

That battens on
Her faltering heart,
Naming her pure,
Elect, apart.

FOUR VISITATIONS

Baucis and Philemon

Life lies to hand in hoe, spade, pruning-knife,
Plain wooden furniture and wattle walls,
In those unspoken words 'my husband', 'wife',
In one another's flesh which still recalls

Beneath the map of age their savoured youth.
It is an ambience in which they move
Having no need to grasp or grub for truth;
It is the still persistence of their love.

That one should die before the other's death
And drain the world of meaning is their fear:
Their hope, to draw together their last breath
And leave the sunlight on a common bier.

Life is the meaning and the bread they share;
Because they need no Gods, the Gods are there.

Semele

I imagine an English Semele –
A gawky girl who strayed beyond the town
Picking at stalks, alarmed by puberty.
Who by the handsome stranger's side lay down

And when he'd gone lay still in meadow-sweet
Knowing herself betrayed into the world –
Soft flesh suffused with summer's placid heat,
The clement light in which the ferns uncurled.

Both faded; meeting him again she sought
For that half-apprehended, longed-for power –
The glitter haunting her distracted thought
That seemed to peer from every leaf and flower,

The glory of the God . . . the girl became
The landscape's ghost, the sunlight's edgy flame.

Jacob I

This mother's darling, picksome in his pride,
Who lives by smiles, deceit, dumb-insolence,
Is sent out to secure a fitting bride
And takes the road in high self-confidence.

By noon there is no road – no shadows move
But his; the desert light glares hard and clear,
A lucid proof that he is owed no love,
That what pervades his solitude is fear.

The young man sleeps, his head propped on a stone,
Exposed to starlight and the vacant skies:
The angels climb, descend, and he is shown
Their ladder's length drawn up from where he lies.

First light, and cold air chills the dreamer's face
Waking to silence, in an empty place.

Jacob II

By sunset they had reached a shallow stream:
The women crossed and he was left alone
Unable to advance. As in a dream
A man with features known but scarcely known

Stood in his path and in the dusk they closed,
Strained sinew against sinew silently:
Who was the stranger whom his strength opposed,
The dark shape jealous of his liberty?

Dawn came, and locked within their stubborn fight
The traveller knew whose arms withheld him there;
'Bless me' he cried, 'Bless me before the light
Dissolves your substance to resistless air'

And one whom strength and skill could not confound
Was forced by benediction to the ground.

ST EUSTACE

At dusk in the dark wood
The stag I'd harried stood –
Its wet flanks flecked with blood

The antlered head held high
As if not he but I
Were hunted here to die;

Between his tines the air
Grew solid to my stare;
The cross of Christ hung there –

I marked where he had bled;
Bright on his thorn-crowned head
The blood shone newly shed –

And as the moonlight broke
Through ash and smothering oak
The dead man moved and spoke.

GETTING THERE

Now you approach the long prepared for place
The language you have learnt, the map you know
Seem childishly inadequate to show
Its obvious, unformulable grace.

But you were told that it would be like this
– An interim, an emptiness – a state
In which, like an expectant child, you wait
Not knowing what it is you must not miss.

'UXOR VIVAMUS...'

The first night that I slept with you
And slept, I dreamt (these lines are true):
Now newly-married we had moved
Into an unkempt house we loved –
The rooms were large, the floors of stone,
The garden gently overgrown
With sunflowers, phlox, and mignonette –
All as we would have wished and yet
There was a shabby something there
Tainting the mild and windless air.
Where did it lurk? Alarmed we saw
The walls about us held the flaw –
They were of plaster, like grey chalk,
Porous and dead: it seemed our talk,
Our glances, even love, would die
With such indifference standing by.

Then, scarcely thinking what I did,
I chipped the plaster and it slid
In easy pieces to the floor;
It crumbled cleanly, more and more
Fell unresistingly away –
And there, beneath that deadening grey,
A fresco stood revealed: sky-blue
Predominated, for the view
Was an ebullient country scene,
The crowning of some pageant queen
Whose dress shone blue, and over all
The summer sky filled half the wall.

And so it was in every room,
The plaster's undistinguished gloom
Gave way to dances, festivals,
Processions, muted pastorals –
And everywhere that spacious blue:
I woke, and lying next to you
Knew all that I had dreamt was true.

TO HIS WIFE

after Ausonius

Let us, dear wife, still live
As we have lived and keep
Those names we learnt to give
When we evaded sleep

On that first blessèd night.
O never dawn the day
When we forgo the rite
By which to you I say

'My girl' and you to me
'Young man'. Though we grow old
As ancient sages we
Shall not grow gravely cold:

Wisdom will be to know
The sweetness of the years –
Unnumbered they shall go,
Unwept for by our tears.

TRAVELLING

You live for landscapes scudding past, the sense
That what sustains you is mere transience;

And for the dew immobile in each dawn –
The one clean stillness everywhere reborn.

A SHORT HISTORY OF CHESS

When chess began in India
The bishops charged as elephants,
The queen was still a minister
And both were clearly combatants

In battles secular and male.
Who claims that Eastern ways perplex?
It took the West to twist the tale
To strategies of faith and sex.

OFF-SHORE CURRENT

Though I'd been warned I once
Ridiculously dived
Into that turbulence –
God knows how I survived.

I could not now repeat
Such glib insouciance
When caution bids retreat –
I didn't catch her glance.

A LETTER TO OMAR

I

I stood beside the ghastly tomb they built for you
And shuddered with vicarious, mute guilt for you;
Are concrete columns what they thought you meant?
I wanted wine, a glass turned down, drops spilt for you.

A sick child reads (his life is not imperilled –
He sucks the candied death-wish of FitzGerald);
I was that child, and your translated words
Were poetry – the muse's gaudy herald.

Was it for you I answered that advertisement
Before I knew what coasting through one's thirties meant?
If so I owe my wife and child to that
Old itch to get at what your Englished verses meant.

Thus in your land I doled out Shakespeare, Milton –
Decided I preferred sheep's cheese to stilton
But knew as much of Persia or Iran
As jet-lagged fat cats sluicing at the Hilton.

My language-teacher was a patient Persian Jew
(I pray that he survives), a techno-person who
Thought faith and verse *vieux jeux*; he thought me weird –
He learnt my loyalties and his aversion grew.

Love proved the most effective learning lure and not
His coaxing tact: my girl required the score and plot
– Explained in halting, pidgin syllables –
Of our first opera (which was – aptly – *Turandot*).

When I had said, in crabbed words bare of ornament,
What *La Bohème*, *The Magic Flute* and *Norma* meant
She married me; my Persian was still bad
But now I knew I knew what 'nessun dorma' meant.

We set up home . . . but I feel more than sure you
Would nod assent to Dr Johnson's poor view
Of tulip streaks (*Damn all particulars* . . .)
And I desist – I wouldn't want to bore you.

2

You left the busy trivia unspoken:
Haunted by vacancy, you saw unbroken
Miles of moonlight – time and the desert edge
The high-walled gardens, man's minute, brief token.

And if I revelled in your melancholy
(Like mooching through the rain without a brolly)
It was the passion of your doubt I loved,
Your castigation of the bigot's folly.

Besides, what could be more perversely pleasant
To an ascetic, hungry adolescent
Than your insistent *carpe diem* cry
Of let conjecture go, embrace the present?

And all set out (I thought so then, I think so now)
In stanzas of such finely-wrought, distinct know-how
They were my touchstone of the art (it is
A taste our pretty *literati* think low-brow).

Such fierce uncertainty and such precision!
That fateful metre mated with a vision
Of such persuasive doubt . . . grandeur was your
Decisive statement of our indecision.

Dear poet-scholar, would-be alcoholic
(Well, is the wine – or is it not – symbolic?)
You would and would not recognize the place –
Succession now is quasi-apostolic,

The palace is a kind of Moslem Deanery,
But government, despite this shift of scenery,
Stays as embattled as it ever was –
As individual, and as sanguinary.

The warring creeds still rage – each knows it's wholly right
And welcomes ways to wage the martyrs' holy fight;
You might not know the names of some new sects
But, as of old, the nation is bled slowly white.

3

Listen: 'Death to the Yanks, out with their dollars!'
What revolution cares for poet-scholars?
What price evasive, private doubt beside
The public certainties of Ayatollahs?

And every faction would find you a traitor:
The country of the Rubaiyat's creator
Was fired like stubble as we packed our bags
And sought the province of its mild translator.

East Anglia! – where passionate agnostics
Can burn their strictly non-dogmatic joss-sticks,
And take time off from moody poetry
For letters, crosswords, long walks and acrostics;

Where mist and damp make most men non-committed,
Where both sides of most battles seem half-witted,
Where London is a world away and where
Even the gossips felt FitzGerald fitted;

He named his boat *The Scandal* (no misnomer...)
And fished the coast from Lowestoft round to Cromer,
One eye on his belovèd Posh, and one
On you or Virgil, Calderon or Homer;

Then wrote his canny, kind, retiring letters
To literature's aggressive, loud go-getters –
Carlyle and others I forbear to name
Who had the nerve to think themselves his betters;

You were the problems (metrical, semantic)
From which he made an anglicized Romantic –
The perfect correspondent for his pen
(Inward, mid-century, and not too frantic);

As you are mine in this; it makes me really sick
To hear men say they find you crass or merely slick;
Both you and your translator stay my heroes –
Agnostic blessings on you both!
                              Sincerely, Dick.

November 1982

EXILES

The two friends fill their time with chess: black plays
Decisively – white dithers and delays,

Picks up a pawn, stares, scowls, then puts it back;
He sees that his spectacular attack

Has turned into a tedious defence.
He cannot win but keeps up the pretence

Of caring how he loses and to whom.
The wives are chatting in another room;

Their rumours rise in disconnected scraps –
'and gold' – 'but X was shot' – 'the prince perhaps' –

'and she got out with nothing, so she says.'
White sees a move that prettily delays

Black's victory... 'my dear, that's just her joke.'
'No, no – she claims she's *absolutely* broke.'

Black pauses now and white turns round to shout
'Sweet, who are you two gossiping about?'

WOMAN ON A BEACH

How mild, how equable, are sun and sea.
The lean, lithe body of my child at play
Is not distinct from its desire, and I
Acknowledge, and inhabit, no desire.

TWO EAST ANGLIAN POEMS

Trattando l'ombre come cosa salda
DANTE, Purgatorio XXI.136

With John Constable

Slow-rotting planks and moody skies;
I look with your impassive eyes

Whose tact is love for what is there —
The worked soil and the moving air,

The reticence of grief: I hear
Through silence your dead voice draw near —

Those words you gave to Ruisdael's art,
'It haunts my mind, clings to my heart.'

Edward FitzGerald

East Anglia, a century ago:
    I see FitzGerald bow
    To Attar's *Conference*
    As I do now

Leaning through silence to a dead man's mind,
    A stranger's pilgrimage
    (As is the book we read)
    To a blank page —

An immanence, remote, but quickened by
    An old, ill scholar's breath:
    I see you wrest this life
    From brother death.

THE TRIBE OF BEN

How easy now to mock
Those who wrote looking back
To rare Ben Jonson's line –
Firm royalists to a man

Unfitted for the claims
Of chiliastic times,
Preferring penury
To the trimmer's smooth way.

Filed epigram and lyric
Held Fanshawe, Lovelace, Herrick
From lazy shame; each sought
In his obscured retreat

Not rage or grief but grace,
An undeluded peace.
Hear how such passion gives
Perfected verse its voice.

A PHOTOGRAPH: TEHRAN, 1920s

How false, incongruous, each prop
That crowds into your photograph —
The stiff, fake flowers, the painted drop
To signal opulence (park-gates
Your shoulder half obliterates),
The draped and tasselled table-top

Against which you benignly lean.
A slight smile ghosts your bearded face
As you confront the strange machine
Which traps you in your mullah's robe
(A signal now that half the globe
Can snigger at and call obscene).

Your gaze holds mine: I know that you
Were never rich, depraved, or mad;
That at your death a rumour grew
Of unemphatic sanctity;
That your frail legend troubles me;
That all the signals are untrue.

RICHARD DAVIS

. . . minding to have sent to Qazvin Alexander Kitchin, whom God took to his mercy the 23rd October last: and before him departed Richard Davis one of your mariners . . .

HAKLUYT, Principal Voyages of the English Nation

Our mariner's last landfall was this shore:
My namesake stood, four hundred years ago,
The empty Caspian at his back, and saw
A shelving view I intimately know –

Clean, silent air and noble poplar trees,
A marshy plain beyond which mountains rise,
The snow-line and the sky – all this he sees –
The colours fresh and calm before his eyes.

Fresh as your fading figure in my mind:
You look back to your little ship, then stare
As if the riches you had hoped to find
Were somehow present in the limpid air.

You walk towards the limits of my sight –
I see you stumble in the dusty light.

ON AN ETCHING BY J. S. COTMAN

I wept to see the visionary man – Dryden's Virgil

    There is no richness in this scene,
No life to answer his abstracted stare –
And what we take it that these emblems mean
Is but the index of his inward care;

    The summer-house will always stay
About to fall, the river make no sound
As Lethe-like it bears his strength away
And lapses to the darkness underground;

    And poised above the silent flood
The couchant lion waits, a mask of stone,
Impassive by the tree that will not bud,
The spell-bound youth, beleaguered and alone.

    The landscape is an open grave
At which the artist and his subject gaze;
When acid eats the plate, his skills engrave
Wanhope, a mind that falters and decays.

CHILDHOOD OF A SPY

Much earlier than most he found
Most things are not as they appear;
The mousy child who makes no sound
Lives in a haze of smothered fear –

Where is he safe? Reality
Is something glimpsed through misted glass;
A closed, adult conspiracy,
A frontier post he may not pass.

Truth is a secret and he learns
Its lonely code; the bit lip trembles
But says nothing – compassion turns
To hatred that a smile dissembles.

The frontier will be down, his fear
A state ubiquitous as air;
And, vindicated, he will hear
Their cry of candour and despair.

NEAR COLTISHALL

for Michael Riviere

Dark on the evening sky
(Though one gleams coldly bright
Caught by the sun's last light)
The thunderous aircraft fly
Into their deepening night:

Distracted from my page
I watch each passing plane –
The virtue of Montaigne
Is innocent to gauge
The wrath that they contain.

O privacy, retreat!
What fastness is secure
From that pervasive roar,
Who shall escape defeat
From what we dream of war?

(The village where I read
Is but a reference
On some chart marked 'Defence' –
Roofs overflown at speed
And of no consequence.)

Which would you choose, my lord –
The cant of government,
The smug cant of dissent?
Or would you turn toward
Your book's long argument

That wisdom is to know
How blindly we descend
To where no arms defend
Our ignorance from no
Imaginable end?

THE RANSOM

after Baudelaire

Man must, to pay his ransom, till
Two dark, rich fields through every season;
The blade that cuts the clay is Reason
Subservient to his patient will.

To make the least rose open there
Or wheat extend its meagre ears
He irrigates with salty tears
The stubborn fields of his despair:

The one is Art, the other Love;
And when the law demands he pay
The ransom due on Judgment Day
Nothing will move the Judge above

But grain heaped in His granary,
And flowers whose loveliness is such
Their mingled forms and colours touch
The angels' hearts to clemency.

MARIAM DARBANDI

1956–1983

How frightened you were once
— And not so long ago —
When late one night we took
Our pathway homeward through
The churchyard where you saw
Grey gravestones row on row;

And afterwards we teased
Your childish, tense alarm
And mocked the way you clung
Against your sister's arm
As if you sensed the dead
Reach through the moonlit calm.

Dear child, I see you now,
Dear helpless fugitive —
To guide you past that place
What could I now not give?
The taint was in your blood
That would not let you live.

Earth holds you in her arms
And soothes you of your fear
And it is we who turn
To see the dead appear;
Who listen for the voice
We know we shall not hear.

READING

The last page read you pat
With thoughtful tenderness
    Your novel's spine –
How much I'm moved by that
Improbable caress
    Which I thought mine.

I copied it from you?
You picked it up from me?
    Who knows which way
The gentle gesture flew...
It marks that privacy
    We both obey.

MY DAUGHTER SLEEPING

Your eyelids are so thin
That as you sleep I see
The eyeballs dart within
That near transparency
Of blue-veined, restless skin.

What do you dream, my dear?
Already after less
Than five quick months your fear
Is fear at which I guess:
I kneel as if to hear

The whispered testament
Of what I cannot know –
My listening head is bent
To silence trapped below
That thin integument.

AUCTION – JOB LOT

    Framed, sepia photographs –
The blank eyes and the awkward pose,
Blurred faces no one living knows –
    These are their epitaphs.

    Closed lives return our stare,
Heaped jumble in a cardboard box:
Curls in a locket that still locks,
    A Book of Common Prayer,

    Its fly-leaf foxed and torn
Through the brief message and the date –
'To Meg, June 1858,
    "In Christ we are reborn".'

    Letters, a faded name,
Dried flowers...Value is of the heart,
The worth we cherish we impart
    And in our death reclaim.

A CHRISTMAS POEM

Written for the 1982 Carol Service of Nene College, Northampton

    One of the oxen said
'I know him, he is me — a beast
    Of burden, used, abused,
    Excluded from the feast —
    A toiler, one by whom
    No task will be refused:
I wish him strength, I give him room.'

    One of the shepherds said
'I know him, he is me — a man
    Who wakes when others sleep,
    Whose watchful eyes will scan
    The drifted snow at night
    Alert for the lost sheep:
I give this lamb, I wish him sight.'

    One of the wise men said
'I know him, he is me — a king
    On wisdom's pilgrimage,
    One Plato claimed would bring
    The world back to its old
    Unclouded golden age:
I wish him truth, I give him gold.'

    Mary his mother said
'I know his heart's need, it is mine —
    The chosen child who lives
    Lost in his Lord's design,
    The self and symbol of
    The selfless life he gives:
I give him life, I wish him love.'

ABANDONED CHURCHYARDS

    The long grass covers
    Untended graves –
Deep in its airy caves
    Drowse summer lovers:

    Flesh is subdued
    To simple needs.
Think, where the rank grass seeds,
    Love was pursued.

HEARING A BALKAN DANCE IN ENGLAND

The music gives itself, retreats:
Your mind's involuntary eye
Dazzles with fluttered handkerchiefs
Against a clear, Levantine sky;
In a quick pause the bride receives
Her groom's first kiss. The phrase repeats,

Repeats; again they dance.
                        And you,
A stranger at the wedding-feast,
Caught up in happiness, were there
Until the circling rhythm ceased –
As now it ceases and the air
Of Norfolk's sky glows Iznik blue.

TRANSLATING HAFEZ

North West Frontier, 1880s
    for V. L. Clarke

I see the man I conjure – at a doorway
Bathed for a moment in the evening light
    And watching as the sun
    Descends behind bare hills

Whose shadow blurs, and renders substanceless,
Parade ground, barrack, flag-pole – the low step
    On which he stands; 'the hour
    Of cow-dust', but no herds

Are brought in here to shelter from the dark:
The bright, baroque commotion of the sky
    Is simplified to dusk
    In which the first stars shine

Like an admonishment that stills the heart.
He enters the dark house: though he is here
    By accident he makes
    His being of that chance,

Set down within a country which he loves
And which, he knows, cannot love him – so that
    His homage is a need
    Become its own reward

Unprized as that which Aristotle says
Souls nurture for the irresponsive God:
    A barefoot servant brings
    The oil-lamp and his books

(And in another dispensation he
Would be that grave, respectful, silent child).
      Moths circle him and tap
          The lamp's bright chimney-glass;

Now seated at his desk he opens text
And commentary; he dips his pen and writes
      'It is the night of power,
          The book of grief is closed...'

EXILE

I turn from longing to the tasks life gives.
Beneath all surfaces your river flows –
I call you Grief. I shun you and I hear
Your murmur as I give myself to sleep.

Lares

ACEDIA

A lumbering, bumpy bullock-cart
Deep in the selfish provinces:
Your mood lurches and sways, over
Ruts, into potholes; you are flung
From side to uncomfortable side.
Goading the beast does no good, nor
Does yelling. It's started to rain.
This would be risible if there
Were someone to share the joke with.

6 A.M. THOUGHTS

As soon as you wake they come blundering in
    Like puppies or importunate children;
What was a landscape emerging from mist
    Becomes at once a disordered garden.

And the mess they trail with them! Embarrassments,
    Anger, lust, fear – in fact the whole pig-pen;
And who'll clean it up? No hope for sleep now –
    Just heave yourself out, make the tea, and give in.

'AND WHO IS GOOD?...'

    And who is good? The man who does least damage?
The saint who labours to transcend the human mess?
Often enough it's some poor conscience-stricken wretch
    Terrified of his own unhappiness.

UNDINE

Evasion led him to a moonlit glade
But she was waiting there and drew him down
To the stream's brink beneath the thickened shade;
White water parted, and her white hair spread
About her body like a billowed gown.
Thin fingers tugged at his; as he obeyed,
Gingerly feeling for the rocky bed
Which was not there, he knew that he would drown
And let his whole weight sink. She kissed him then,
Her gentle mouth on his sucked out his breath
Which he was glad was gone. He did not hear
The liquid trickle of her laughter when
She broke alone into the air, or fear
The sudden depth where he encountered death.

MIDDLE EAST 1950s

This is a revolutionary photograph –
The crowded faces stare beyond the frame.

All but one: he looks into the camera,
An anonymous, middle-aged man holding
His daughter who turns her back to us, pressing
Her curls against his shoulder. Behind them
Soldiers gesticulate, crowded on a tank.

How open his face is: you read there hope,
Fear, decency. You see what is betrayed.

IBN BATTUTA

Near the beginning of his first journey
The great traveller (who was to suffer
Shipwreck, the loss of all his wealth, his slaves
– On whom he doted – and his son; who was
To fight with pirates, brigands, be received
By princes as an equal and be laughed at
As a pauper; who was to see the known world
And its wonders) near the beginning
Of his first journey he tells us how
In company with a caravan of travellers
He approached a city, and how a crowd
Of well-wishers and relatives came out
To welcome them, so that each man was greeted
By a face he knew, except for him,
Ibn Battuta, whom no one greeted
Because he was a stranger there, and how
This knowledge was borne in on him, and how
He wept.   When the book is closed this picture
Of the young man in his twenties weeping
– And not the princes, slaves and shipwrecks –
Is what stays with you
              so that you almost feel
Across the centuries the pressure of
Your hand against his arm, and hear
Your own voice raised in greeting.

THE DEPARTURE OF THE MYTHS

Now that the series of
Tottering bedizened
Edifices goes toppling
And tinkling into
The distance, surrounded
By singers and saltimbanques,
By outriders who curvet
Their horses and flourish
Bright, fabulous weapons –
We cannot deny that
The silence is (as
They grinningly warned us
It would be) unnerving.

But almost immediately
It's broken; a child
Is wailing somewhere –
And look, there it is
Grubby and rubbing its eyes,
About five years old,
Of indeterminate
Sex, left behind by
The glamorous, vanishing,
Self-absorbed caravan that
Now, as we watch, grows small
In the sunset.
          Suddenly
We see how ridiculously
Heedlessly cruel
That gross splendour had become –

How could it have touched us?
We hate it and rush
To console the distraught
Child who stubbornly
Evades our caresses and
Bawls for its mother.

EVENING

At the lawn's edge the wood
Promises solitude.

Wet, tangled undergrowth
Has crept across the path

Where fox and badger go
Oblivious of you.

This is unhappiness
Where you must not trespass.

Turn back to the bright house,
Your child asleep upstairs,

Her face illumined by
The night-light's quiet glow.

HOUSEHOLD GODS

Not books and pictures, no; although their sense
Must be the context of benevolence.

And not, no not, 'the sweepings of bazaars',
The clutter of our different, dying cultures.

Moments, not objects; the impalpable
Embodiment of what we hope is real.

The children's clothes untidy on a chair;
Voices absorbed in what they know and share.

The house silent at night, unspoken love.
Your book slips down; you sleep and do not move.

Lares; the bits and bobs of privacies,
Scraps, trivia; the heart's allegiances.

Devices and Desires

JEALOUSY

To hear her talk about her friends
Is like glimpsing across dark gardens
Their lighted room, from which you are
Excluded; such kindness reigns there
In the bright warmth; you see a burst
Of laughter that you cannot hear.

Or it is being shown a blurred
Photograph of some unreachable
Good place: *look, there are olive trees
And the beach where we swam – we slept
In that white house* . . . You finger it,
The glamour of a life not yours.

WISDOM

The common wisdom is 'Accept what's given':
What's given is a long unhappiness,
A purgatory that cannot lead to heaven.
And O yes we accept it, more or less.

WITH JOHNSON'S *LIVES OF THE POETS*

for R. L. Barth

He wrote these quick biographies
To be instructive and to please;
   In them we find

Among judicious anecdotes
The apt quotation that denotes
   A taste defined

And wrested from this record of
His irritable, captious love
   For failed mankind –

From fear, from his compassion for
Insanity, the abject poor,
   The world's maligned.

He laboured to be just, and where
Justice eluded him his care
   Was to be kind.

Read generously – as once he read
The words of the indifferent dead.
   Enter his mind.

JANET LEWIS, READING HER POEMS

The tape begins. A few pages are shuffled
Then her voice is there – old now, clear, unruffled,
Unassertive, going again among
Words given order when the heart was young:
The cadences are like that vanished race
They would evoke, leaving almost no trace
On the after air; gentle, evasive,
Too modest to accuse or to forgive,
Declaring simply this was here, and this,
Which is gone now – the bright frail edifice
Of summer stripped in time's storm.
                                    But I share –
As the tape plays – her sense of sunlit air,
Of glades where uncoerced humanity
Knew wisdom as a kind of courtesy.

TO THE MUSE

I can't complain
If you disdain
    To visit me –

Too often I
Tried to deny
    Your quiddity;

'She is a way
With words,' I'd say –
    'A competence

In what we make.'
A fool's mistake.
    My punishment's

To see you now –
Dark eyes, smooth brow,
    Your slim form turned

From me; cold, real,
Inviolable.
    Well, I have learned.

MAGIC

The child steps carefully
    Over the cracks
And at the corner sees
No bears – he can relax.

Grown older now, he says
    It's childish rot
But pulls white petals off –
She loves . . . She loves me not.

The next step is to cheat:
    'If I can climb
That hillside in an hour,
If I can find the rhyme

I need, she loves me' – and
    He does; but she
Doesn't. This is the Fall
Into Contingency;

He puts such magic by,
    Walks carelessly
Toward the messy future:
His poems do not rhyme.

MAKING A MEAL OF IT

No point in murmuring
Against the life you live,
No point in hungering
For what Fate cannot give;

No point in calling up
Vast, empty words like Fate –
The table's set, sit down
And eat what's on your plate.

THE SENTIMENTAL MISANTHROPE

You get things clear, define a space,
And find you hate the human race:

But act *gemütlich*, let things slide,
And it's yourself you can't abide.

MADE IN HEAVEN

They bring to one another what they are
Which is obscurely what was done to them:
The poise of the angelic predator,
The blank hunger that cannot say *Amen*.

HERESY

This is your heresy –
To translate and displace.
Your long desire to see
Salvation in a face

Unstable as your own
Is to be blind to what
Is literal blood and bone;
To worship what is not.

AFKHAM

I wanted otherness
And met your gaze, in which the world shone unreproved;
You were the world itself,
The uninterpretable strangeness to be loved.

A Kind of Love

LADY WITH A THEORBO

c. 1675, John Michael Wright
Columbus Museum of Art, Columbus, Ohio

Daily I visit you
As if you needed me;
We're strangers here, it's true,
Divided by the sea
From England, home, the place
We both grew up in once,
But that's not what I trace
In your still countenance,
Still and demurely young,
Untested yet by life
Not knowing how you're strong,
A daughter, no one's wife,
Protected, loved, and yes
Awkwardly beautiful.
English, but I would guess
Part something else as well —
Italy's there perhaps
Or Spain; I'll never know.
Resting across your lap's
Expanse the huge theorbo
Dwarfs you, and now you'll play
Breaking the silence where
I gaze at you each day,
Saying you want me there,
Not knowing how to name
My longing not to leave
You in your worn gilt frame:
Call it a kind of love.

QATRAN

In Tabriz I saw a poet named Qatran, who wrote decent poetry, but he could not speak Persian well. He came to me and brought the works of Manjik and Daqiqi, which he read aloud to me. Whenever he came across a meaning too subtle for him he asked me. I explained it to him and he wrote it down. He also recited his own poetry to me.

TRAVEL DIARY OF NASER KHOSROW (11th century)

Poor Qatran, with your just passable verses
And provincial Persian, with your eagerness
To construe the poets you'd pored over.
You watch your distinguished visitor as he
Rides out of the gates and your life, leaving you
At the roadside, in the dust, but grateful for
His urbanity, his kind condescension,
His smile as you read from your masterpiece.
You stand for a moment, a little nonplussed,
As if something else could be said, but he
Doesn't glance back, and you fade from our sight.

SOCRATES' DAIMON

As if he shared the heron's awkward grace
Alive to every ripple of the stream
And focused for the flicker, the dark trace,
The sudden stab that breaks the sunlit dream,

He sees the darkness underneath the light:
UnReason whispers in his head the rule
That men are most wrong when convinced they're right:
He will cajole them into Reason's school.

FATHERHOOD

O my children, whom I love,
Whom I snap at and reprove –
Bide your time and we shall see
Love and rage snap back at me.

'OUTSIDE THE SNOW...'

Outside the snow, and winter sunlight fills
The convalescent's room, where a fire is lit.

He remembers his delirium – the storm
Of rage and grief, the pit of self-reproach,

All horrors that the past provides; but now
The cat kneads his stretched out body with her paws.

As sleep envelops him he's conscious of
The flickering and the ticking of the fire

Which tells him he is safe until he wakes.

THREE VERSIONS OF THE MAKER

Pygmalion, the shaggy-fisted brute,
Wooed Venus, who — as might have been expected —
Smiled, told him she felt flattered, and rejected
The lout's embarrassingly frantic suit;

He sulked and set to work, sculpting her form
In ivory (the bits he couldn't see
He carved the way he wanted them to be)
And took her into bed and kept her warm.

She stirred against him in the dark: Dear Jove,
He thought, Desire's unhinged me, I've gone mad . . .
But no: the nicest night he'd ever had
Made Shaggy-Fist an adept in sweet love . . .

This is the cosiest version.
                              Moslems say
That if you make a figure you must give
Its lifeless form the wherewithal to live
Or be forever damned on Judgment Day,

Which isn't so attractive — though it's clear
This anagogy's likelier to be true
Than lucky Shaggy-Fist's: if what you do
Lacks life both it and you will disappear.

But the most desolate is this: the doll
Kokoschka made in hatred of mankind
And took into his solitude. Its blind
Pupils stayed blind; he loved the lifeless loll

Of limbs and neck, their jointed artifice –
He could not bear the puppet-bitch to live:
Her stubborn stillness was her beauty – and if
He could he would not wake her with a kiss.

DISCIPLINE

Such hunger, such unhappiness...
Who said, way back, true discipline
Would cure it? You bought that for a while
And intermittently still do.

What disciplines then! Languages
And verse... most exigent of all
The always being somewhere else,
Familiar unfamiliarity,
A life held briefly as the image
Quick in a stranger's eye: look, she
Appraises you and turns away.

LEARNING A LANGUAGE

    Correctly, she repulses you.
Blushing and mumbling, what would you not do
    To make her difficulty yours? –
Her tongue quick in your mouth like a glib whore's.

ARGHAVAN

In England it's a Judas Tree
And here a Red Bud. For us though
It must keep its Persian name –
Which for their poets means the glow
Of spring, and youthful modesty.

To see it growing by our door
The winter that we wound up here
Seemed like a portent of good luck –
In spring we watched the buds appear
And felt less outcast than before.

MOHSEN: A GARDENER IN CALIFORNIA

If asked, he'll pause from vacuuming the leaves,
Push back his frayed straw hat, and itemize
His past for you.
                An Arab, born in Iraq
When the British ran it, sent at eighteen to
Cold Moscow where he studied hard to be
An atheist, an engineer, an exile.

Then home again, to intrigue, politics,
Betrayal, the sudden bloodbaths of the 60s,
Escaping with his life and not much more;
Trieste and Sao Paolo where he learnt
Italian, Portuguese . . . until he heard
They'd let him be that undistinguished thing,

An immigrant who puts himself through college –
New York, and farthest West, to California:
The grand finale was a Ph.D.
In physics . . .
              But now a slackening of the will
Removed him from that scramble, and he took
Odd jobs, slowed down, got married, learnt to garden.
To be content, to raise his children who
Are ignorant of all the Old World's truths –
Of Arabic, blood-feuds, the past: who are
Nice California kids.

          An abrupt pause
In which he smiles and hands on hips surveys
The garden with a quick professional eye.
As if it were an afterthought he lists
The things he knows about himself. He's learnt
A gallimaufry of new languages
That half persist and when he thinks they're gone
Emerge unusably in pointless dreams;
He knows he loves, distrusts, the grandiose claims
Men make for science, and for poetry
(O yes, he writes, in Arabic of course);
He knows he's no one's fool, and that he can
Survive.

          A longer silence. He must go.
Another garden waits for his attentions.
He packs his tools into his van, grins, waves.

When he is gone you sense, if only for
A moment's space, unspoken histories,
The lives of wanderers who wind up here,
Each with a past that seems unthinkable.
They learn to trust what they are grateful for –
The stillness and the space; the light (you could

Be in the Middle East, it is so pure,
So crystalline and imperturbable);
The peace; the perfect blue of sky and pool.

ON THE IRANIAN DIASPORA

You've seen a child intent on carrying
A cup brimful of water from the sink
– Step by careful step – to the kitchen table,
And then triumphantly sit down to drink.

This is the task the exile undertakes;
The heavy cup he balances is full
Of reminiscence and desire – the depth
In which he sees a world before the Fall.

He walks a narrow corridor where strangers
Jostle the vessel he cannot refill,
He sees the liquid that his life depends on
Lurch in his trembling hands, and spill, and spill.

There is no table where he could set down
His awkward, emptying charge; his stiff arms ache;
As there is less to drink his thirst increases;
It is a thirst which he will never slake.

Touchwood

'TOUCHWOOD: *decayed wood . . . used as tinder.*'

TO 'ESHQI

1893–1924, Iranian poet, murdered by his country's secret police

I'm someone who you wouldn't want to know.
If I had met you eighty years ago
Before my birth, your death, I hardly think
That we'd have trusted, even sensed, the link
That I sense now, in reading you, between
Your youth and mine – too much would intervene.
My accent would be just a goad to you
To spit, or run, or tell me all you knew
Of England's avarice and treachery.
I've heard that mix of fact and fantasy
And met your avatars so many times,
Sat listening to the litany of crimes –
Been patient, lost my temper, smiled, agreed,
And always recognized that clawing need
To spell the rape out once again, to say
'We were your helpless and dismembered prey.'
I'm used by now to acting out the son
The fathers' sins are visited upon –
Imputed sins or true, it's all the same:
The ache is real enough, and so's the blame.

What could unite us then? What quirk could span
The chasm cast between an Englishman,
A wandering subject of that nation state
Your patriotic confrères love to hate,
And you whose life was given to the fight
To free all Asia from imperial might?

First there's the wandering – like me you spent
Long years in self-elected banishment,
In cities where your language was a way
To discount everything you had to say,

To mark you as a parasite or worse –
Was this the prod that pushed you into verse?
The sudden sense that language is a maze,
That meaning mystifies, that sound betrays?
And then the sense that if this sense were true
You might as well exploit what threatened you?
Above all, words themselves, and poetry –
I see in you what I once felt in me,
A kind of drunkenness for what the past
And language lend us, and which will not last,
A pointless love for sound and sense allied,
Bequeathed by all the poets who have died.
And there's the feeling too your young verse gives
Of one who's fearful of the way he lives,
Who's hounded by the thought of death, whose need
For it is like a harsh erotic greed –
Till revelling in your grief you prophesied
That soon enough you would embrace the bride:
A murderer's bullet made your rhetoric
Appear as sober as arithmetic.

By contrast my more circumspect flirtation
With Thanatos avoided consummation:
But still your verse revives for me that sense
Of self-inflicted psychic violence,
A mayhem of the spirit that destroyed
My youth and left a suicidal void . . .
Enough of that; that I survived is due
To someone like and wholly unlike you.

Are these enough then? Verse and exile, death,
Common humanity; shared, human breath?
Why should I look for a response from you?
Why should I care? No words can now undo
The violence of your life and of its end,
And what can reach you from a would-be friend?

Not language, not these verses that I make
In spite of silence for your verses' sake:
Dear poet, here, too late, is sympathy,
Late friendship from a helpless enemy –
An unavailing monologue, but made
In homage to your absent, angry shade.

A MONORHYME FOR MISCEGENATION

for Yass Amir-Ebrahimi and Stuart Benis

We all know what our elders warned
In their admonitory drone,

'Water and oil won't mix, my child –
Play safe, stick staunchly to your own.'

And I concede they're half right when
I think of all the pairs I've known

(Black/White, Jew/Gentile, Moslem/Me –
The home-raised with the foreign-grown):

Mixed marriages, it's true, can make
Two lives a dire disaster zone.

But only half: since when they work
(As my luck, and my friends', has shown)

Their intricate accommodations
Make them impossible to clone:

For gross, *gemütlich* kindness, for
Love's larky, lively undertone,

For all desired and decent virtues,
They stand astonished and alone.

GIVEN BACK, AFTER ILLNESS

    Again after absence
You are home, but weak, chastened,
Come now to be cherished
Among flowers and our children,
As loved and as longed for
    As they were new born.

    Again after absence
You're beguiled by such beauty,
But worn now and wasted
In a world too unwieldy,
Wanting sleep and long silence
    For hour after hour.

    Again after absence
Your head presses our pillows
And I wake by your profile
Cut clean as a coin's face,
There to breathe in the breath
    You frailly exhale.

AFTER THE ANGELS

Once the angels had dispersed
Diaphanous into
The starry nebulae,
Men asked the animals
For versions of themselves.

So many choices waited:
Loners and lethal packs,
Slow vultures, sly hyenas
That scavenge other lives,
Grand solitaries like
The bear that never seeks
Its kind except to mate,
The spider spinning death
For all unwary insects,
Cold-water fish that dive
Into the darker depths
Loving the icy reaches,
If we can call that chill
Beyond all passion love.

And there were those like us
Who scavenged too, for comfort —
Anthropomorphic, schmaltzy,
Happy to see the monkeys
Defleaing one another,
Cuffing, hugging, their babies.

Happy to see two ducks
Bobbing downstream from us
Alert for scraps we throw them,
Their movements weirdly twinned
Together and together,

Solicitous and greedy,
Snapping up what's offered –
The pretty mandarin ducks
That pair off once, for life.

STILL

Still after twenty years I keep
    Love poems by the bed,
Still when I wake from wandering sleep
    A child's unfinished dread

Empties my body and I turn
    To see your sleeping face –
Wise with a wisdom I can't learn,
    Trusting, giving, in place.

YOUR CHILDREN GROWING

You see your own face with another mind
And then your own mind with another face;
You and not you, too raw, then too refined,
A shameful sameness and a stranger's grace.

COMFORT

Insomnia: I get up, read, then write,
A bit of consciousness alone at night.
The house is cold; after an hour or two
I stumble back to darkness, warmth and you.
You are asleep but as I gingerly
Edge into bed, you turn to welcome me:
No comfort I have known in any place
Can equal that oblivious embrace.

INTO CARE

Here is a scene from forty years ago:
A skinny, snivelling child of three or so

Sits on a table, naked and shamefaced.
A woman dabs his body to the waist

With yellow pungent ointment and he feels
Her shock as she remarks, 'Look at the weals

On this boy's back.' Her colleague steps across:
Gently she touches him. He's at a loss

To think what kind of 'wheels' she sees, but knows
That here at least there will be no more blows.

PRAGMATIC THERAPY

Old childhood traumas must come out they say –
Dig down, prise loose, let in the light of day.

You found a rusted nail stuck in a door,
Tugged, wrestled with the pliers, fumed and swore

Until it snapped – and left a jagged pin
Lying in wait to snag unwary skin.

What could you do but bang it home? You hit
The thing with all your strength and buried it.

TOUCHWOOD

Quirks of lost childhood give
The fears by which we live,
And look – identity
Is like this twisted tree
The lightning struck at there,
Till for a dry, warm lair
The woodlice entered it:
In secret, bit by bit,
They make a mealy bin
Of touchwood sealed within.

ANTHONY 1946–1966

Brother, now that you are dead
And live only in my head
Where your life is as the sound
Of deep water underground
Moving with its steady roar
Like the silence we ignore
As the given of our being,
As the daylight to our seeing;
Brother, though there is no way
You can hear the words I say
Still through more than twenty years
I ask pardon for your tears –
For the grief that bludgeoned you
And the death it dragged you to,
Knowing, now you cannot live,
You cannot forget, forgive,
Knowing unforgiven I
Must live on and fear to die.

A PHOTOGRAPH OF TWO BROTHERS

How old were we? Eight, ten or so?
I seem the tearful one – you glow,
All bounce and boyish confidence,
Which looking back now makes no sense.
I haven't changed that much – and yes,
I hurt too easily I guess,
Though mostly now the tears I shed
Are proxy tears, for you, long dead.

THE SUICIDE

Here is the punishment, the condign shame,
The frightened child unravelling through the years;
Here is Rejection and the Parlour Game
Whose rules say 'Everything must end in Tears.'

AFTERSHOCKS

At nervous intervals
    You feel the pain again,
A jolt of recognition
    Coming God knows when;

And though each time you see
    The tremors have diminished,
You know you'll never say
    'They're over now; it's finished.'

MAY

Late in the evening light
Grass verge and hedgerow glisten
With one unvarying white;

White cow-parsley below,
Above white hawthorn blossom;
Who in this dusk could know

Where weed to flower gives way,
Or when their ghost releases
The last light of the day?

GOING HOME

What can be called evasion?
Is it to go away?
Or to ignore the world
And like a limpet stay

Stuck to the self-same rock?
Whichever you decide
– Resistance to the waves,
Surrender to the tide –

What you will not evade
Is doubt accusing you
Of infinite evasion
In all you say and do.

A SASANIAN PALACE

The great hall at Firuzabad
    Lies open to the weather –
I saw two adolescents there
    Playing chess together.

There was no splendour to distract them;
    Only a cavernous shade
Cast by the drab and crumbling vault
    Where silently they played.

So much of Persian verse laments
    The transience of things
And triteness was mere truth as they
    Pursued each others' kings

Where kings had given orders for
    Armies to march on Rome,
And where I watched their game awhile
    At home, and far from home.

FLIGHT

After the Arab defeat of the Persians in the seventh century AD *some aristocrats of the defeated Sasanian dynasty fled to China. Gravestones indicate that they hung on there as a distinct community for at least two centuries.*

In time the temporary withdrawal
Became a way of life. How long
Before they could admit there'd be
No going back, before they ceased
To live off rumours of a prince,
A scion of the royal house
In hiding, living hand to mouth,
About to gather troops to hurl
The haughty enemy back from
The gates of Ctesiphon –
                which was
A pilfered ruin, a harmless tourists'
Curiosity somewhere beyond
The brave new city of Baghdad?

So they erect the stone inscribed
With words that speak to home though home
Has long since ceased to speak such words,
A witness to a way of life
Corroded by fidelity
That is a kind of willing madness;
A story told and then retold,
Whose referents are all elsewhere,
And now lives only in these minds
That still repeat the litany
Of what was lost, till they too die.

GOLD

Its atavistic glitter will not fade
And that's the point: barbaric power and pride
(Piled torques and rhytons gaudy in a grave)
Point to the presence of what lived and died.

Thin gold paint flaking where the panel rots
Beneath a saint's robe and a Duccio sky
Signal not merely bourgeois amour-propre,
But hope that something of us will not die.

Take it as frozen threnody, a sign
Of avid and abashed humility,
Of human failings fined down to the wish
To lodge a fragment in eternity.

MIRAK

Mirak, descendant of the Prophet, born
About the middle of the fifteenth century:
An Afghan brought up to the family trade
Of bow-maker, who as an adolescent
Turned to reciting the Qoran, was soon
A praised professional at it, tried his hand
As a calligrapher and thence became
The painter of all painters, the miniaturist
To end them all, the Wonder of the Age,
The unsurpassed whom kings sought out, who sketched
From life – while travelling, while a guest at banquets,

Untroubled whether courtiers crowded him
Or left him to his own absorbed devices;
And to the admiration of his time
Was never seen to use an easel. A man
Whose passion when not painting was for wrestling
(Each day he lifted weights to build his strength)
At which, of course, in due course, he excelled.

A talented young orphan came to him
To be apprenticed as his servant, page,
Paint-mixer, gofer, sweeper-up, a boy
To trace and prick the pounces; now and then
Allowed to colour inexpensive pieces.
This was Behzad, whose teacher Mirak was,
Whose fame eventually eclipsed Mirak's
And whose pure, sumptuous, gentle miniatures,
So bright with passion, whimsy and restraint,
Are now the art's unrivalled masterworks
While not one solitary sheet has been
Attributed with any certainty
To Behzad's quondam teacher – Qoran reciter,
Bow-maker, calligrapher and wrestler,
Mirak, surpassed (perhaps) at last, unheld
By any trade, adept at all he touched,
Patient for mastery but negligent
When once he had the mystery in hand:
Or so we picture him, at this blurred distance.

NAMES

In *Inghilterra* you imagine love
  Voluptuously fair,
A Verdi tenor's voice, the wedding rites
  Of Melos and Despair:

In *Inglistan* exasperated hate,
  A certainty that spies
Corrupt the patient labours of the Just
  With smiles, and gold, and lies:

In *Britain*, as the Mid-West says the word
  (And how much more in *Brit*)
Bemused contempt, respect, a sense that They
  Were, and now We are, It.

And *England*? Childhood's word? Your first flight starts:
  As toy-town falls away
Fear, longing, a voracious hope undo
  Whatever you might say.

WE SHOULD BE SO LUCKY

Here is a shameful, strong
    Nostalgia – to have been
A minor functionary
    At some resplendent scene,

A man trained up in skills
    And complicated rules,
Leaving small room for genius
    And even less for fools,

Someone who knows exactly
    How and what to do,
Who works discreetly, knowing
    Others know this too.

A journeyman musician
    Grimly fuming at
His self-important patrons'
    Catatonic chat;

A portrait painter able –
    Happy – to revoke
Defects of nature with
    A defter, softer stroke;

Or best, court panegyrist,
    Where a perfect rhyme
Might mean a pension paid,
    Perpetually, on time.

MASTERS

When I was prick-sore young, God knows,
Loose Eros led me by the nose
(Disguised at times as Tenderness
Or worship of pure Comeliness,
But underneath such glozing dress
Lascivious Eros nonetheless).

But now that he's renounced my service
And taught me what polite reserve is,
Am I improved in any way?
– Led by Scholastic Vanity,
Bland, treacherous Timidity:
God give me Eros any day.

TENURED IN THE HUMANITIES

Now he can live and work among
Those who skim books to write their own,
Who thousand-cut another's tongue
To wag their trophies, clone to clone;

Who when they read are sure that they
Know more than authors what words mean,
Who never opened Rabelais
Though (naturally) they've conned Bakhtin;

Who when they write rewrite their betters
With crowing malice and contempt,
Who mean to trash the mind and letters
(Though they themselves will be exempt) –

A lumpen mob that occupies
The palace and the stable yard,
Whose chief joy is to organize
A long and lucrative *noyade*.

NEW READER

He reads, rewriting as he goes – it's just
    A timeless bar-room scene:
'Don't give me that crap,' the bully yells,
    '*I'll* tell you what you mean.'

ART HISTORY

Paintings and poems – what survives,
The residue of used-up lives
That want to live a little more.
Their gaze pursues you to the door.

Your life's an orphanage in which
The foundling poor stare at the rich
Who load their arms with children they
Hug briefly – but then walk away.

EPITAPH

This erstwhile traveller's
    Become a tourist –
Bring out the fake folk knick-knacks,
    He's no purist.

Serve him his own cuisine
    With an ethnic grin –
Nirvana for him now's
    A Holiday Inn.

COUPLES

I

Breakfast is brusque and when it's done
Her life without him's rebegun;
She's typing, on the phone, her looks
Say 'I'm preoccupied, these books —
And so much else — need seeing to,
I haven't time to glance at you.'
And all the time what fills his head
Is how she turns to him in bed.

II

Her friends all told her how much he admired her
And naturally she thought that he desired her,
But though he read the books she recommended,
Though her views were the ones that he defended,
Though he accompanied her to exhibitions,
Bought CDs of her favourite musicians,
And proved a prudent person to rely on
For movies, shows, a shoulder there to cry on
(Yes, even that . . .), the move for which she waited
(Expectant, disappointed, then frustrated)
Just never came: and then by God it hit her
(Few truths we have to swallow taste more bitter):
'This bastard who pretends to be so kind
Despises me — he only wants my mind.'

OLD COUPLE

'How much they do,' the neighbours say,
'So kind in any, every way –

So quick to help and never ask
Why they should shoulder one more task.'

Not knowing all they do is for one
Long dead, for whom too little was done.

MIDDLE AGE

I

We miss out; we don't mind; we make less fuss.
Living? Our poems can do that for us.

II

Life with no bloom of newness to it;
But, surely now, you always knew it –
That this was how it was to be:
Old friends invited round to tea
At which the rude young are deplored
And no one yawns or says, 'I'm bored.'

REPENTANCE

'I won't do that again,' you say. We'll see.
Tomorrow is another day. Feel free.

DESIRE

A myth that you believed in once, it's gone
And you can't credit that you've been so stupid:
Damn the whole crew you say, damn Venus, damn
Her sparrows, damn her little bastard Cupid.

A TEASE

    She'll simper and say, Yes – and go
To meetings hubby never quite suspects,
    At which she'll simper and say, No –
Who needs adultery without the sex?

A QASIDEH FOR EDGAR BOWERS ON HIS SEVENTIETH BIRTHDAY

Nasib

X years ago a would-be poet wrote
His mental mentor an egregious note –
Not something of the kind that rock-stars get
(Since he was British and they'd never met)
But still a letter from a serious fan,
Too pushy maybe, glibly partisan
(Of course he sent his own slim volume too
And crossed his fingers, as one never knew...):
A cautious note came back – sober, polite,
Gently encouraging the neophyte.

Goriz-gah

I was the jittery, determined fan,
And you the prudent poet; so began
A friendship that has meant as much to me
As any in my nano-Odyssey.

Madh

In Santa Barbara on the well-walked beach,
Talking technique, too moderate to preach
But sure in your perception of the line
Where chaos meets and modifies design;

Qasideh: a praise poem, conventionally in four unequal sections.
Nasib: introduction. *Goriz-gah*: transition. *Madh*: praise.
Du'a': prayer for the object of praise and/or for the writer.

Or in your room, to me a magic place
Where waves unwove their constant thorough-bass,
A cave of making with an ocean view,
Die Zauberflöte and *The Tempest* too;
Or visiting my family and me
In England where you helped a native see
His homeland with a foreign friendly eye,
Discerning, undeceived, distinctly dry;
Or in Ohio where I write this letter,
Insisting that what's central *can* be better,
In concerts and museums, restaurants, zoos
(These last you seem unable to refuse),
A dear companion with an eye and ear
For all that's complex, marvellous, austere
Or simply filled with an unruly charm –
Whatever will delight and do no harm.
I could not list the things you've taught me here,
The music, paintings, poems, prose – the sheer
Accumulation of delicious stuff
That's in my head because you cared enough
To pass it on – nor could I list the ways
Your casual kindness constantly outweighs
The claims of friendship. Knowing you has been
(And may it be for years yet unforeseen),
To steal a phrase, a liberal education,
A cause for gratitude and celebration.
And if I'd never known you there'd be cause
For more than this inadequate applause
In all you've written – in the poems I
Was all those years ago bowled over by
(My *vade mecum* now and known by heart
They stay my perfect image of the art);
And how much more so in your latest verses
Whose unobtrusive, faultless skill rehearses
Our species' exaltation, need and loss
'Fastened by love upon the human cross'.

Du'a'

I wish you well then, now you've reached the age
It seems appropriate to call you sage –
I doubt sagaciousness will keep you from
The pleasures you pursue with such aplomb,
I hope not anyway. And I trust too
The muse continues to call in on you
And that you'll entertain her and pass on
The gossip that she brings from Helicon.

IN PRAISE OF AUDEN

God knows it's possible to fault you
    But of whom worth his salt
And our perusal is this not a given?
    Besides we have to live
Cum grano salis, just as we read you,
    And lives too, like art, can need
Their moments of pure inspired zany.
    For me at least the dull pain
Of our past and present is both conjured
    And distracted by the fun
You so generously heap on our platters,
    A hostess whose old hat
Is outlandish but whose heart beats gracious
    In the spot-on right place.

The cliquey tics that irritated
    Swelled up at a compound rate –

Your campiness and giggly mania
    For the outré and arcane
(I owe *sessile* and *soodling* to your nudges,
    Though a surfeit's like girl-scout fudge
Each meal for a week till one breakfast
    We gasp out, 'Dear hostess, a break!')
Then there's health and religion – two areas
    In which I firmly don't care
To place myself under your tutelage,
    Though glad to be your pupil
In this, if a lollygagging, laggard
    One, now verse is my bag.

How much though you knew, and saw through us ...
    The schoolmaster's rage to you
Was a small boy's tears, the tyrant's mad gesture
    Nostalgia for the breast
Of mother, O mother, whose Isolde
    You once were to her bold
But decorous Tristan: and how your words waken
    Weeping childhood where we shake
In the grip of the ogres' grand nightmare,
    Bereft of all love and light.
How right too you proved when the doors of Europe
    Slammed to at the word Jew –
Our clerisy's conscience and so branded
    A betrayer of England.

My praise is for decency, craft-lore,
    The twin ways you laughed
Off what wouldn't depart, importunate
    Self-important Fortune,
The hand dealt you by orgulous Duty;
    You could be rude and cute
At the drop of a hat and often
    Were, but the sidelong cough

Of Conscience recalled you always to
    The one life that pays,
As, minding our manners and metres,
    You affirmed the discreet
And distinguished; in cosmic terms a trifle,
    But an unwasted life.

SUZANNE DOYLE'S POEMS

The bitter power your poems concentrate
Is like the wines they love to celebrate —
Acrid and sharp, a dark embodiment
Of feral life and earthly sediment,
A tart explosion to the taste and brain
That leaves us reeling and a touch insane,
As if we drank down blood, not something made
By an archaic, honourable trade —
Which is the triumph of the trade, to make
What's tricky and impossible to fake
As wrenching as a hurt child's sudden cry,
As simple as the fact that we will die.

A TRANSLATOR'S NIGHTMARE

I think it must have been in Limbo where,
As Dante says, the better poets share
Old friendships, rivalries, once famous fights
And, now they've left it, set the world to rights.
As I was being hustled through in transit
To God knows what damned hole, I thought I'd chance it
And chat to some of the assembled great ones
Who looked as bored as trapped theatre patrons
Who've paid good cash and find they hate the show...
I picked on one: 'I rather doubt you know...'
He started up and peered at me: 'Know you,
You snivelling fool? Know you? Of course I do!
You ruined my best poem. Look who's here...'
He turned to his companions with a sneer,
'Traducer and destroyer of our art,
The biggest stink since Beelzebub's last fart.'
They jostled round, each shouting out his curses,
'You buried me with your insipid verses...'
'You left out my best metaphor, you moron...'
'You missed my meaning or they set no store on
An accurate rendition where you come from.'
'He comes from where they send the deaf and dumb from,
He got my metre wrong...', 'He missed my rhymes',
'He missed puns I don't know how many times,
Then shoved his own in...' But I turned and fled,
Afraid that in a moment I'd be dead
A second time, torn limb from spectral limb.

A mist came down and I was lost. A dim
Shape beckoned; thinking it must be my guide,
I ran for reassurance to his side.
But it was someone I'd not seen before,
An old man bent beside the crumbling shore

Of Lethe's stream. He stared a long time, then
'Did you translate?' I screamed, 'Oh not again!'
But as I backed off one quick claw reached out;
He clutched my coat and with a piercing shout
(He didn't look as though he had it in him)
Cried, 'We've a guest! Who'll be the first to skin him?'
Then added, 'Just my joke now; stay awhile,
The crowd in these parts is quite versatile,
Though we've one thing in common, all of us:
When you were curious, and courteous,
Enough to translate poems from our tongue
All of us gathered here were not among
The chosen ones.' I looked around – a crowd
Now hemmed us in and from it soon a loud
Discordant murmur rose: 'Please, why not mine?'
'You did Z's poems, my stuff's just as fine . . .'
'The greatest critics have admired my verse . . .'
'You worked on crap that's infinitely worse
Than my worst lines.' '*Some* of my stuff's quite good –
You will allow that? – It's not *all* dead wood?
Why then . . .?' and slowly the reproaches turned
To begging, bragging, angry tears that burned
Their way into my sorry soul.

                        Once more
I ran and saw my guide, tall on the shore
– The other shore – of Lethe. 'Rescue me!'
I called, 'Get me to where I have to be
For all eternity . . .' He smiled: 'My dear,
You've reached your special hell – it's here, it's here.'

LATE

A glass of wine (the third or fourth tonight)
And Hafez read by fire- and candle-light.

Act Two of *Tristan*. As the record plays
German and Persian merge in *Sehnsucht*'s haze.

Now firelight, music, poetry combine
To bless the mind already blurred with wine.

FIREFLIES

The children run in the garden
Catching at fireflies,
Blue smoke from last year's leaves
Pricks at the eyes.

So brief the light and leaping flames
No need to tell the moral –
Quickness and beauty nag at the heart
With the old quarrel.

Belonging

SHADOWS

The sun comes up, and soon
The night's thin fall of snow
Fades from the grass as if
It could not wait to go.

But look, a lank line lingers
Beyond the lawn's one tree,
Safe in its shadow still,
Held momentarily.

Delighted my daughter runs
Twisting from my embrace
To touch the fragile snow
Before it leaves no trace.

A MONORHYME FOR THE SHOWER

Lifting her arms to soap her hair
Her pretty breasts respond – and there
The movement of that buoyant pair
Is like a spell to make me swear
Twenty odd years have turned to air;
Now she's the girl I didn't dare
Approach, ask out, much less declare
My love to, mired in young despair.

Childbearing, rows, domestic care –
All the prosaic wear and tear
That constitute the life we share –
Slip from her beautiful and bare
Bright body as, made half aware
Of my quick surreptitious stare,
She wrings the water from her hair
And turning smiles to see me there.

HAYDN AND HOKUSAI

Masters of wit and line
Who welcome what is ugly,
Lumpish, disproportionate,
And give it grace, distinction –
Whose humour is a pool
For all of us to splash in
(And we emerge like angels
Double-dipped in Pactolus
To shimmer in bright air
That is and is not earthly. . .)

Haydn and Hokusai,
Who say to Anguish 'Go!
Out! *Retro me Satanas!*'
Though you, and more than most,
Have seen its rodent eyes
Burn in the icy dark,
And felt the fetid blast
Of dragon breath assail
Your heart, hearing the slaver
Of wide hyena jaws –

Haydn and Hokusai
Be with me now, lighten
My lumpen moods, drive off
Ungainly panics, spleen,
Purge me of selfish torpor;
Remind me that you loved
Life's dailiness, its quirks
And frumpish joy; and that
If there is heaven on earth
It's here, it's here, it's here.

NIGHT THOUGHTS

For some, and maybe the majority,
    I know reality
Means what preoccupies their waking hours –
    But not for me

For whom the real is not light's rapid rush
    Of chance and change, day's crush
Of difficulties, duties, deals, distractions –
    But the still hush

Of darkness where my grateful mind has grown
    One with the monotone
Of whispered breath beside me where you sleep
    Embraced, alone.

IRAN TWENTY YEARS AGO

Each summer, working there, I'd set off for
The fabled cities – Esfahan, Kashan,
Or Ecbatana, where Hephaestion died,
The poets' towns – Shiraz and Nayshapour,
Or sites now hardly more than villages
Lapped by the desert, Na'in or Ardestan . . .

Their names now mean a dusty backstreet somewhere
Empty and silent in the vivid sunlight,
A narrow way between the high mud walls –
The worn wood of the doors recessed in them
A talisman to conjure and withhold
The life and lives I never touched or knew.
Sometimes I'd hear a voice, a radio,
But mostly there was silence and my shadow
Until a turn would bring me back to people,
Thoroughfares and shops . . .

                              Why is it this that stays,
Those empty afternoons that never led
To anything but seemed their own reward
And are more vivid in my memory
Than mosques, bazaars, companionship, and all
The myriad details of an eight year sojourn;
As if that no epiphany, precisely,
Were the epiphany? As Hafez has it,
To know you must have gone along that way;
I know they changed my life forever but
I know too that I could not tell myself
– Much less another – what it was I saw,
Or learnt, or brought back from those aimless hours.

TO THE PERSIAN POETS

for Sarah Johnston

What rights have I, trespassing in your rooms,
Pilfering your lines, sifting your sacred dust,
Searching for what you were and are not now?
As if I came to where Achilles flickered,
Drawn by the blood Odysseus spilt for him.

But, in another tongue, a stranger speaks,
The revenant who shows me what I am:
In whose hermetic words I recognize
The animals and angels of my heart,
My happiness, my longing, my despair.

POLITICAL ASYLUM

My closest friends were killed. I have a life
That's comfortable in almost every way.
I haven't got a job yet, but my wife
Has found a good position with good pay –

Enough to keep us going anyway.
I don't go out much but, you see, my wife
Is out for almost all of every day.
I read a lot and reassess my life.

I've tried to write, but what is there to say?
My friends were killed and this is now my life;
It's almost certain this is where we'll stay.
We like it here, especially my wife.

IN HISTORY

In history there never was a land
With no-one there before we entered it,
Neither God's promises nor Lebensraum
Lay listless for the taking: so we carved
On others' faces our predestined map,
And when the voice of God receded, blood
Was on our hands and in our eyes forever.

GÓNGORA

(whose father was an assayer of goods confiscated by the Inquisition)

The new world's gold – searched out, expropriated –
Brought home in squat, pot-bellied caravels;
Pain clung to it, pure, unobliterated
And found new halls of anguish, older hells:
Reworked as filigree and massy plate,
Sword-hilt, menorah, monstrance, crucifix,
Prized objects of virtù, rich gifts of state
Bright with the promise of apocalypse.
A child pokes through them in a lumber room
(His silent father's writing at a table):
Worship and fantasy, and puissant Spain;
Imagined glory gores the velvet gloom.
Violence and glamour tell their lying fable
To one who has no notion now of pain.

A PETRARCHAN SONNET

for David Caplan, who told me that the Marquis de Sade was a descendant of Petrarch's Laura

Here's a coincidence to give one pause:
The poet's perfect paradigm of grace,
Laura's unreachable, dissolving face,
Proleptically, with no overt applause,
Becomes the ultimate, unconscious cause
Of lust's eponymously saddest case:
A prison cell's a fine and private place
For Onan's simple, solipsistic laws.

Justine joins Laura's shade in Paradise
And punishment's the price of Liberté,
Not only Petrarch burns in fire and ice,
Not only Laura looks and looks away:
Self-murdered in their dreams of sacrifice
Marquis and Poet shudder and obey.

CASANOVA

Con-man *extraordinaire*, grand cabbalist
Whose angels spell out Leporello's list,

Antaeus who draws strength from touching hearts,
And better-guarded, more lubricious parts;

Shape-shifter, trickster, miracle-producer,
Braw bobby-dazzler, all-the-world seducer,

Commoner, snob, suave crony at the palace,
Ruled only by your own unruly phallus . . .

High on the Doge's roof you slip, flail, crawl –
But our appalled applause won't let you fall.

DIDO

Remember me, but ah! forget my fate . . .

Aeneas leaves to found his nation-state
And all that we remember is your fate:

The tinsel's torn, transmogrified desire
Extravagantly feeds the fatal pyre;

Your putti scream; then, smudged with smoke, escape
To publish love rewritten now as rape;

And in the gulf the breeze that fills his sails
Wafts to his ears their penitential wails.

IN THE RESTAURANT

A Queen in exile, she presides at table,
Her weather-eye on rowdy merriment;
Her rule seems easy, even negligent,
But all the family knows her glance is able
To quell or swell the boisterous friendly Babel
That swirls about her, tamed and turbulent:
A Cybele you'd say, embodiment
Of all that's customary, tribal, stable.

Who, seeing this plump matriarch, could guess
That thirty years ago she'd risked her life
To cross Beirut's bomb-cratered no man's land,
Defying anguished parents, to say 'Yes'
And be an unbeliever's outcast wife,
Careless of who'd condemn or understand?

DUCHY AND SHINKS

for Catherine Tufariello and Jeremy Telman

Duchy and Shinks, my father's maiden aunts,
Lived at the seaside and kept house together:
They bicycled in every kind of weather
And looked across the waves to far-off France.
Routine had made their days a stately dance,
A spinsters' *pas-de-deux*, with every feather
Where it ought to be: no one asked them whether
They liked a life with nothing left to chance.

They showed me photographs of long ago –
Two English roses in a chorus-line:
I said, 'They're lovely' as I sipped my tea.
They were too – at the *Folies*, second row,
Or down-stage, glittering in a grand design,
With every feather where it ought to be.

WEST SOUTH WEST

Since I was born in Portsmouth, west south west
Would mean the Solent, then the open sea:
A child let loose on Nelson's Victory
I fantasized his last quixotic quest,
Trafalgar's carnage – where he coolly dressed
As gaudily as if he wished to be
The natural target for an enemy,
And willed the bullets to his medalled chest.

Hardly a gesture I could emulate.
My west south west was more a stealthy game
To be elsewhere, escape, rewrite my fate
As one who got away. But all the same
I find I walk the shattered deck and wait
For when the marksmen see me, and take aim.

TERESIA SHERLEY

Waking in the Sussex dewfall with the first light showing through
Hearing English rustlings, stirrings, as the day begins anew,
Grateful for surprise, survival, for my exiled life with you

As my lawless mind betrays me and I'm neither here nor there,
Neither bride nor wife nor mother, still sublimely unaware
That there was a place called England, that we had a life to share –

So in no place I lie hearing sounds that give me to the past,
Wagons creaking, kitchen clatter – but I know the dawn has passed
And no call from dawn's muezzin told me night had gone at last:

Still I stay here for a moment not consenting quite to wake,
Over Esfahan's green gardens I remember morning break,
Yellow light on pools and plane trees, and the shadows that they make

And the sudden breeze of sunrise, like a nervous lover's hands
Hardly touching, but still touching, as my body understands,
Like a whisper that insists on life's importunate demands

Tugging me to love and pleasure, to what passes as we sleep,
To the roses' quick unfolding, to the moments that won't keep,
To the ruin of a childhood, and the tears that parents weep.

When you begged my hand in marriage and the shah gave his consent
Gossip called me Christian payment or a pretty compliment
But I'd seen you and considered what a marriage with you meant –

Strangeness always my companion, at my side and in my bed,
Unknown syllables exulting in my mouth and in my head
Silences I couldn't fathom, all my faux-pas left unsaid.

But what's marriage but a launching of a life to the unknown?
Whether yoked to some poor dervish, or the partner to a throne,
Women's lives stay inextricably dependent and alone:

And the glamour of your difference was rubbed amber to a straw,
As I trembled like a mouse beneath some cat's capricious paw
Barely breathing 'Yes' when asked if I approved of what I saw.

If the hazards I accepted were no worse than others choose
Still I feared my life without you if it seemed I might refuse –
All the ways I could be left alone with nothing left to lose,

So I came to you, became your wife and, as you said, your friend,
Ignorant of everything – except my nagging need to spend
All my days within the dream-life I could not allow to end.

Promises proliferate; an alien in a curious land,
Drawn to lives I thought I'd be a part of, love, and understand,
Clutching at what can't be closed on by a fumbling foreign hand –

This I shared with you, my darling, when I saw you lost, unsure
As the conversation chanced on turns you hadn't bargained for,
As Rejection smiled urbanely, and Discretion closed the door,

Left you what you were, a stranger, and you saw – whatever *you* did –
Though the phantom Friendship beckoned, smiled and simpered,
    she eluded
All attempts to hold her: you stayed welcomed, baffled, and excluded.

This we shared in Europe, fêted in Vienna, Prague and Spain
As the entertaining envoys of the shah's exotic reign,
While the gaudy greetings withered to politely phrased disdain –

And the Vatican, remember, when beneath St. Peter's dome
We were gawked at as the cicerones' chic-est sight in Rome,
Dogged by strangeness till we rested in the place that you call home

Where you looked in vain for childhood that you'd thought could
 never change
And you realized that from now on life at best could rearrange
Vistas lived through, and abandoned, and irrevocably strange.

This we shared then, and we share it, and for this I let my eyes
Open on the pallid half-light that I daily recognize
As the emblem of my exile . . . but the harsh nostalgia dies:

Neither Persian, no, nor English, as I see dawn's light erase
Dearest darkness and its phantoms . . . and I'm ready now to face
All of morning's minor duties, all that's weirdly commonplace.

WHAT

Now that the soul's become
A nervous zero-sum,
Something the cortex's
Pavlovian synapses
Produce by accident –
A blur, a taste, a scent,
That seems to (but does not)
Refer back to a what . . .

What is it that your gaze
Locked on my face conveys?
And whose is the colloquy
Of silent sympathy
I share in seeing you?
What is it makes us two
Indivisibly whole,
Dearest, if not the soul?

'A WORLD DIES . . .'

A world dies when a person dies; who sees
And savours life as he did who is dead?
No one now lives the myriad privacies
That made the life that ends, now, on this bed.

'SWEET PLEASURE...'

Sweet Pleasure my dear, I haven't forgotten
    The vows you delectably made
To stay with me always, come summer, come winter –
    But it was your sister who stayed:

She winked at me, elbowed me, shoved me aside,
    Then trashed every plan I had laid –
A permanent lodger who calls herself Duty,
    A raucous and boorish old maid.

HIBERNATION

Now that you've gone, and I can't contact you,
I try to live as curled-up dormice do:

Summer's dissolving sweetnesses sustain
The little limbs and heart and dreaming brain,

And I too live off what I stole and kept
From summer foraging, before I slept.

NO GOING BACK

     My mother loved deep voices –
Paul Robeson, Kathleen Ferrier – rich,
     Romantic, with the weight
Of tragedy about their lives,
     Odds overcome, succumbed to;
The sob she heard reverberate
     In every note they sang.

For recreation I put on
     High sexless voices – Emma
Kirkby, or some nameless counter-
     tenor whose life I'm happy
To ignore – kidding myself I cruise
     Their cloudless stratosphere;
Transcendent, bright, no weight, no tears.

SECRETS

A family full of secrets, of the kind
Well-meaning folk now call dysfunctional;
We always moved but never left behind
The memories we were not allowed to have.

Anguish and pleading and indifference
We each of us played all the rôles in turn;
It seemed eternally to make no difference
But we were wrong since one of us was dead.

I ran away to books, fantastic lands,
To verse, where things add up: I came on Rostam
Floundering in the pit his brother's hands
Had dug, pierced by the stakes I knew I'd sharpened.

OUT OF TIME

I woke with sorrow in my mind
    For no apparent cause
And could not see why I should be
    Subject to sorrow's laws;

All day my life seemed out of time,
    Nagged by a nameless pain
I could not trace to any place;
    Still it usurped my brain –

Omnivorous and intimate,
    Growing insistently
Till by day's end it seemed a friend,
    A fate, a part of me;

Then in the dusk I recognized
    The day I fear and know;
Grief had not lied, my brother died
    On this date, years ago.

AUBADE

for Joshua Mehigan

These are the dawn thoughts of an atheist
Vaguely embarrassed by what looks like grace:
Though colours don't objectively exist,
And have no form, and occupy no space,

So that the carpet's sumptuous dyes must make
Bold arabesques untrue as Santa Claus,
And all Matisse's pigments are a fake
Fobbed off on us by intellectual laws,

Though neither Fauve nor Esfahan survive
The deconstructed physics of our seeing –
Still we consent, and actively connive
In their unreal adjustments to our being.

So the thin rhetoric we use to cope
With being so peculiarly here,
Which cannot but be based on baseless hope
And self-constructed images of fear,

Serves to interpret what we are, although
We hesitate to say that what it says
Refers to anything that we could know
Beyond the mind's perpetual paraphrase.

And sensing that no quiddity remains
Outside the island sorceries of sense
(Queen Circe's simulacra in our brains
That make and unmake all experience)

Still, still we long for Light's communion
To pierce and flood our solitary gloom:
Still I am grateful as the rising sun
Picks out the solid colours of my room.

A SE STESSO

As if sheet lightning struck from empty skies:
Incredulous, afraid, you recognize
The way the world's transformed before your eyes.

You have no right to welcome or refuse
Terror and grace that are not yours to choose,
And what you cannot grasp you cannot lose.

Live in the aura of your luck and bow
Before the brilliance that engulfs you now:
It is not yours to hold, or disavow.

'LIVE HAPPILY'

Le pauvre enfant, il ne sait pas vivre

After a while your mind's a *macédoine*
Of muddled poems, stories, paintings, music,
And pointed admonitions by the dead
Who seemed to know what they were saying meant.

In all this incommodious welter one
Phrase comically recurs for me, the flourish
With which Domenico Scarlatti ended
The dedication of his published work –

'*Vivi felice*' . . . '*Vivi felice*',
Which I've not done yet, or seen clearly how
I'd manage to. Time's running out, his bright
Arpeggios remind me . . . running out . . .

GUIDES FOR THE SOUL

Who thickens from the shadows as you die?
Who silences your comprehending cry?

Emblem of all you lost and now inherit,
What psychopomp attends your parting spirit?

The unattainable belovèd who
Usurped your life once, and eluded you?

The worshipped clerisy, your sacred dead
Oracular inside your dreaming head?

They may be there – lost somewhere in the host
Of those who welcome your convulsive ghost.

It is a crowd that parts for you, a throng
Among whom now, forever, you belong –

They are the pleas you had no patience for,
The pathos you brushed off: the waiting shore

Is filled with those you failed. You recognize
The sum of what you are in their blank eyes.

GAMES

What metaphor is adequate?
What image makes a baggy fit?
    What trope
    Might cope?

Floods behind levees rising higher
Smooth as a psychopath's desire,
    Until
    They spill?

Termites devouring from within,
Till wall and floor are merely skin
    And all
    Will fall?

The grinding of tectonic plates?
What power, when mass on vast mass grates,
    Could halt
    Earth's jolt?

Nothing so gross or grand you say.
But now that every (every!) day
    Confirms
    That worms

Or fire will feed on you – and soon –
What's the appropriate slow tune?
    The phrase
    Which says

That you, for all your games, for all
You might describe, invoke, recall
    Or cherish,
    Will perish?

VICTORIAN

Dearest, I'd hoped to hear from you today
But Posty had just one for me – from James
(Dear loyal James, who always has to play
On my side in the family's fun and games):

He says that India's indescribable,
And then describes it. He keeps out of harm's
Way, learning Persian verbs. If you still call,
I must convey to you his 'Best Salaams'.

I've often wondered if his funny nose
Might sniff us out. He'd shield us for my sake,
Then preach at me in private I suppose.
I know he thought that Charles was a mistake:

The vulgar sermons grated on his nerves
As now they grate on mine. Can it be true
A woman always gets what she deserves?
Charles is quite sure it's so. As if he knew.

I'm sorry that the last time you were here
The girls distracted me. But Florrie's six
And needs me even more than you my dear –
I can't keep track of all her impish tricks.

And now my Emily has turned fourteen
She's far too pert for Missy to control –
She's *quite* grown up (you know dear what I mean).
Missy's a jewel, but has a servant's soul.

I must go now. I'll try to write more later . . .

Friday. Still nothing from you, dearest love:
I hover round poor Posty like a waiter,
I can't think what he thinks I'm thinking of.

My life's made up of Duty, Hope, and Boredom:
You and dear Charles both think I haven't tried.
It's true I dream about what he'd call 'whoredom'
(Sitting, demurely naked, at your side –

Is that so bad? – and far away from here).
Charles is so good, I ought to be content:
But darling, honestly, you've no idea
How stultifying life is since you went.

I know you hate this kind of talk . . . I know . . .
But sometimes I'm afraid you're tired of me.
I'm not like you, I can't just come and go,
Bird-like, in your belovèd Italy . . .

I can't, and yet I must, live on without you.
Send poems, darling. Don't be angry. Please.
I won't, I mustn't, nag at you or doubt you.
Have pity on your lonely friend. Louise.

A MIND-BODY PROBLEM

We've always been inseparable, it's true,
But don't think that implies I'm fond of you;
I get embarrassed by the things you do –

I feel I can't quite trust you anywhere
And everywhere I go you're always there:
No one could call us an attractive pair.

I think you put my friends off: is it spite
Makes you insist on looking such a fright?
Face up to it, you're not a pretty sight.

And then you have the insolence to claim
That I'm the one who's actually to blame,
That I'm responsible for our shared shame

And if I'd paid attention years ago
And worked with you, and not been so *de haut
En bas*, things would be fine. Well, maybe so;

Whatever, as you'd say, you slob. But I'm
Aware you're contemplating pay-back time,
And punishments appropriate to my crime.

Already I can't sleep too well: vague aches
Won't go away, a doctor's visit takes
Forever and she says, 'for both our sakes',

(Though this well-meant advice is hardly new)
That I should take much better care of you.
You have the upper hand now. As I knew.

JUST A SMALL ONE, AS YOU INSIST

The stuff to soften girls and turn the boys on
In vino veritas – clink – name your poison

What makes parochial differences concur
In one accessible miasmic blur?

The potentate's potations and the peasant's
Admit both rankless to the genial presence

Where torchlight, moonlight and the brashest neon
Reveal what can't be said but all agree on –

Kindness, knowledge, solace, our glimpse of glory...
Tomorrow though is quite a different story.

DESIRE

The bored house cat Desire likes novelty
And has to check it out – goes sniffing where
She has no business to, extends a paw
By way of tentative experiment,
Pats, and withdraws, pretends indifference,
Then pounces. Something valuable could be
In pieces soon. Think, Kitty, what it is
That curiosity accomplishes.

FAREWELL TO THE MENTORS

Old bachelors to whom I've turned
    For comfort in my life,
I find you less than useful now
    I've children and a wife;

And though you're great on *Weltschmerz*, loss,
    Lust, irony, old age,
I draw a blank when looking for
    Advice on teenage rage;

On sibling rivalry and rows
    I can't begin to rate you,
You're silent when it comes to screams
    Of 'Dad, I really hate you'.

So get you gone Fitz., Edgar, Wystan,
    And dear old Housman too;
It's clear that at this juncture I
    Need other guides than you.

A BIT OF PATERNITY

To tell your weeping child
'This too will pass, believe
Me, I've been here before'

Is to be one who walks
Communing with himself
Along a wintry shore

And thinks his murmured thoughts
Might calm the crashing waves,
The winds' inhuman roar.

KIPLING'S KIM, THIRTY YEARS ON

There's an accent he can't place,
There's a meaning that he misses,
There's a charming foreign face,
Quick caresses, whispered kisses.

There's a sari out of place,
There's his conscience (that's his Mrs),
There's a future he can't face,
(Money's mumbling, kiddies' kisses).

NEW AT IT

'You'd like some candy-floss?'
      What child would say, 'No'?
She peers entranced into
      The small volcano

Above which I, self-consciously
      Sixteen, preside.
Six eyes sixteen, then hugs
      Her mother's side.

'Give him your pennies then.'
      She counts them, one
By one, into my palm;
      One more; she's done.

I wave off wasps, then pour
      Dyed sugar in
The little crater till
      It starts to spin:

She steps back, but returns
      As filaments
Cobwebby, cloudy, pink,
      Ever more dense

Collect about the cane
      I glibly twirl
Within their sticky web.
      'Who's a good girl?'

I ask, offering the cloud,
    (No one else makes it
More stylishly I think):
    Gravely she takes it.

DÉJÀ LU

I read my first book through again,
The poems of my messy twenties:
The stench of misery rose up,
Every last stanza stank of it.

And at the time I thought I'd been
So circumspect, impersonal,
Threading my way through myths and metres . . .
I'd never do that now of course.

GROWING UP

What changes is the notion life will change;
It won't cohere at last or come out right,
And no perspective renders where you are
The midst of anything but your disquiet.

OLD

When I was young I wondered
How men zig-zagged and blundered
Into the bile and rage
That enervate old age.

What nags now at my mind
Is how they keep so kind,
Given the blows they bear,
And justified despair.

SMALL TALK

At the Reception

Oh look, there's What's-his-name . . . No, that's *my* drink . . .
And he's important these days, isn't he?
The Times gave him a good review I think.
I'm sure he'd love to read my poetry.
You know him don't you? Can't we go and mingle,
And you could introduce me as your friend?
I'll slip my ring off. There, I'm almost single.
This blouse works pretty well if I just bend
A little forward, no? That's sure to get him.
Well, go on then. Oh who's that awful blonde?
He'd notice me if only she would let him . . .
I wish that I could wave a magic wand . . .
Hey look, she's gone. Come on . . . Why hi! He*llo*
I'm such a crazy fan of yours you know.

Checking Out While Checking In

The bored and beautiful receptionist
    Who's sick of being nice to jerks
Gives me her 'Welcome-keep-your-distance' smile;
    What gross injustice . . . But it works.

The Business Man's Special

The pretty young bring to the coarsely old
Réchauffé dishes, but the sauce is cold.

Et in Arcadia Ego

(ON TEACHING CREATIVE WRITING IN SANTA BARBARA)

A house was rented for the visitor
    Who came to lecture here for one spring quarter:
In house and class his only duties were
    To feed the humming birds with sugared water.

Overheard in Khajuraho

Tier upon teeming tier the friezes rise
Of sculpted couples variously entwined,
And tourists gaze with unbelieving eyes
On yoni, lingam, breast, and plump behind.

I didn't hear her question, but the guide,
Respectfully, and gently as a lamb,
Bends to the blue-rinsed matron at his side
And says, 'No, mosques are slightly different, ma'am.'

JUST SO

Despite their highly paid positions
Prince Esterhazy's picked musicians
Resented being asked to share
His Schloss stuck miles from anywhere:
Pining for their domestic lives
They brooded on their absent wives
Till Papa Haydn gave the Prince
The broadest of patrician hints,
And by his Farewell Symphony
Procured their longed-for liberty.

Just so, eight centuries before,
A hardy central Asian corps
Of cavalry who'd had enough
Of forays, fights, and living rough,
Turned to the poet Rudaki
Whose sweet euphonious eulogy
Of Muliyan (the little stream
That bounded home) broke their lord's dream
Of conquest . . . and returned the band
Abruptly to their native land.

Here is one use for artistry:
The insubstantial filigree
Of singing words or wordless song
Can bring us back where we belong.

A Trick of Sunlight

'THE HEART HAS ITS ABANDONED MINES...'

'The heart has its abandoned mines...'
Old workings masked by scrub and scree.
Sometimes, far, far beneath the surface
An empty chamber will collapse;
But to the passerby the change
Is almost imperceptible:
A leaf's slight tremor, or a stone
Dislodged into the vacant shaft.

CHÈVREFEUILLE

In a neglected glade
The hazel sapling's shade
Quickens with early spring:
New tendrils clutch and cling –
A honeysuckle twines
Its tentative thin vines
Reaching now in, now out,
Above, below, about,
Till intricate, strong strands
Clasp like a myriad hands.
Love's leaves and limbs conspire
As if unsaid desire
Could intimately tether
Their substances together
And none could separate
Their growths' complicit state.
Bright in the summer sun
Two tangled lives are one.

GETTING AWAY

Once, when I was a child of seven or eight,
I turned a corner on a wooded path
And saw a fox a few feet from my face.
We stood stock-still and took each other in:
Instinctively, I looked down at his paws;
He stared at me a moment, then he turned

And loped away downhill, between the trees,
Unhurried, but inexorably gone.

His paws had all been there, I'd counted them,
And so he couldn't be *that* fox, the fox
Some serious grown-up had described for me,
The one whose inadvertent paw had stepped
On steel that sprang shut, snap (the man had snapped
His fingers), just like this: he gripped my arm,
Then asked how brave I was. Could I have done
What that fox did? He'd gnawed the fur and flesh
Down to the bone, imagine how that hurt,
Then cracked the bone, chewed through the lot, and so
Escaped, leaving the keeper only this:
And here he'd slipped a paw into my hand,
Soft, small, and lifeless, with no blood on it.

There was another story I was told
Around that time, which in my mind belonged
With that hallucinatory, bad moment.
The village churchyard had an ancient grave
Whose slab had moved, so that a gap had opened
Through which the darkness showed. One moonless night
A group of scallywags had dared each other
To run and put a hand beneath the slab.
One had agreed, and, as the others waited
Crouched down beside the churchyard wall, they'd heard
A terror-stricken scream, and run off home.
The next day their companion was discovered:
When he had turned to join his friends, a branch
Had snagged his jersey's sleeve, as if a hand
Reached out to hold him, and his heart had stopped.

The fox then or the boy: which would I be?

WATER

Stirred by the charm and beauty of your voice
I lost for moments at a time your meaning:
My mind reached back some thirty years to where
A small stream pulsed between Italian rocks.
High somewhere in the Apennines I saw
Clear water bubbling from an unseen source:
Light glinted on it like a minor blessing,
An inexhaustible sweet iridescence –
Redundant beauty spilling endlessly,
That in another form I drink from now.

HAPPINESS

The weirdest entry in our lexicon,
The word whose referent we never know –
A river valley from a Book of Hours
Somewhere in southern Europe long ago.

Or once, to someone walking by the Loire,
A trick of sunlight on a summer's day
Revealed the Virgin in rococo clouds:
The peasants in the fields knelt down to pray.

HÉRÉDIA

French was his mother's voice, sweet, close and warm,
Muffling the Spanish of their vast estate –
Their backwater baroquely out of date,
Time's flotsam from a long-forgotten storm.
Latin and Greek sustained him through the swarm
Of present truths his heart could not translate.
Paris would distance them: there the debate
Would poise contingency against pure form.

Paris returns the febrile compliment
And her Academician seeks the sea;
Sated with Rome and with the orient
He walks the barren cliffs of Brittany,
Gazing across the formless waves to where
The huge sun sinks beyond Cape Finistère.

THE MAN FROM PROVINS

(*as related in Joinville's chronicle of the crusade of Louis IX*)

After Damietta fell, I pitied them
As one might pity any wretched prisoners;
I saw too what I'd been, friendless and filthy,
Emaciated, sick, a foolish failure.

My friends said I should parley with their king
And though I was concerned I'd jeopardize
The life I've built up here, a kind of guilt,
Or curiosity, or something worse,
Persuaded me to be their dragoman.
You should have seen their faces when my voice
Betrayed that I was French like them, or had been.

I don't know what I'd hoped for. What I got
Was royal anger and a show of horror,
The usual rhetoric of new arrivals,
Made sharper by that piety of his,
Of which his hangers-on are all so proud.
But holy horror's of no use to me:
I left him in his tent, relieved to stand
Back in the sunlight where a man can see things.

Then one of them, as if to make amends,
Came out, and caught my arm, and questioned me,
Eager to know exactly where I'd come from
And why I'd stayed. I told him bluntly then
I was from Provins, famous for its fairs,
A place that had been rich, a handsome town
Perched on its hill above the fertile plain,
Become a haunt of beggars and stray dogs,
No building going forward, and the young men,
Or those who had their wits about them, leaving.

Why should I long for that? I've vineyards here,
A noble house, and other men's respect,
Besides which I have now acquired two things
I love in my ungainly, foreign way:
The language of my neighbours, and a wife.

He asked me urgently about the faith
Which he insisted was still mine, or should be;
I answered him as seemed appropriate,
So that he left believing what he wished to.

BEFORE SLEEP

Let me not lie here, mulling the day's anger,
Rehearsing, if there have been such, its tears;
Let no bitterness beckon, envy linger;
Save me from Circe's, Medusa's, cruel stares.

Let me slip to Sleep's Kingdom unencumbered
By guilt I don't need, by guards who would ask me
For visas I've lost; let me enter unhindered
To where I'm at home: let no one suspect me.

May Kindness take charge then, to see that I'm dipped
In Oblivion's warm baths; and when I emerge
Let me wander Love's island, as one who's released
Unscathed from Doubt's dungeons, manumitted, at large.

THE OLD MODEL'S ADVICE TO THE NEW MODEL

Artistic license isn't all it's painted:
It's true he sometimes wants to move to passion
Before you've had the time to get acquainted,
But that's just flattery or arty fashion.
Take it from me, you won't spend much time rolling
Across the floor or in his bed: his gazes
Are usually less carnal than controlling,
And after all these years what still amazes –
Well, me at least – is how what he's created
Can look like Lust Incarnate's drooling doting
And Lust is what he's certain he's defeated.
If you want that, you'll finish up with nothing.
It's painting he gets off on – that's his pleasure;
He'll paint, but probably not want, your treasure.

EDGAR

i.m. Edgar Bowers, 1924–2000

A few things that recall you to me, Edgar:

A stately '80s Buick; hearing a car
Referred to by a coaxing sobriquet –
'Now come on, Captain, don't you let me down.'
French spoken in a conscious southern accent;
An idiom calqued and made ridiculous
(*'Eh, mettons ce spectacle sur le chemin'*).
'Silly', dismissive in its deep contempt,
'Oh, he's a silly; an amiable silly,
But still a silly.' Or the words I first
Encountered in your captious conversations,
'Tad', 'discombobulated', 'catawampus'.
The usage that you gave me once for 'totalled' –
'Oh cruel fair, thy glance hath totalled me.'

Most recently, in Cleveland's art museum,
The French medieval tapestries brought back
Your unabashed reaction to their beauty,
And how, for once, you'd stood there almost speechless,
Examining Time's Triumph inch by inch,
Enraptured by its richness, by the young man
Proud in his paradisal place, until
You saw what his averted gaze avoided –
The old man, beaten, bent double by fate's blows,
Driven from youth's charmed, evanescent circle:
And how you'd wanted to be sure I'd seen him.

LISTENING

Sweet Reason rules the morning – what's as sweet as
Rosalyn Tureck playing Bach partitas?

Midday's for Haydn, who loved everyone
(Except that pompous pig Napoleon) –
Music's Hippocrates ('First do no harm'),
An *Aufklärung* of common sense and charm.

Mozart and Schubert own the afternoon –
High spirits and a Fiordiligi swoon;
A sudden key change: you will die alone.
The shadow that you stare at is your own.

Then comes the night. Pandora's lid is lifted,
Each scene implodes before it can be shifted –
Longing's a tenor's accurate bravura,
Sex and Despair are *Fach* and *Tessitura:*

And heaven's where the mind's sopranos sing
In harmonies undreamt of in *The Ring*.

WHAT I THINK

On your advice I saw a shrink
Which did me no damn good at all.
She seemed to be the missing link.

I thought she'd calm me, help me think,
And be the David to my Saul . . .
On your advice I saw a shrink;

Substantial as a tiddlywink
Her IQ was Neanderthal,
She seemed to be the missing link.

I thought we'd iron out a kink
Or two, or fight, or have a ball,
(On your advice I saw a shrink);

Perhaps, once, she was on the brink
Of saying something sensible . . .
But no, she was the missing link.

Blandly we skated round the rink,
And didn't jump, and didn't fall.
On your advice I saw a shrink
But didn't find the missing link.

THE SCHOLAR AS A NAUGHTY BOY

Conceive of history as a crumbling palace
Run by a lord both arbitrary and callous;

A little boy peers down between the banisters
And lobs imaginary teargas canisters

Then pokes about in semi-Stygian gloom
Ransacking treasures in the lumber room;

Scuffed velvet, shattered ormolu, stained pages;
The cast-off junk and wisdom of the ages.

Bats flitter, vermin litter, spiders skitter;
Down there the statesmen coruscate and glitter.

ANGLAIS MORT À SANTA BARBARA

Rejoicing in his accent (oh he could sweetly coo it,
And charm the wealthy widows, and didn't mind who knew it) –
They said he went to England, every summer, to renew it.

As never-to-be-vulgar was his peculiar vulgarity
His manners caused his cronies much behind-his-back hilarity,
But as he's gone for good now, why be churlish with our charity?

The morning mist burns off the shore, but this time not for him.
In darkness he is lying still. His eyes, forever dim,
Cannot peruse his Betjeman, or favourite Barbara Pym.

THE SCEPTIC

The people who discuss their other lives
Are utterly unfazed by questions like
'But where do all the extra souls appear from?'
They mutter something about animals,
And quickly change the subject to the fact
That they were once the Empress Josephine,
Or Balzac, or the best friend of St. Thecla.

Small children with a box of dress-up clothes
Enthusiastically try on new lives:
The princess and the pirate preen themselves
Before their gesturing peers, all glamorous,
All brave and loved, their rags turned into riches.
There's always one who gets a little wistful,
Tearful even, unsure what he should wear.
Occasionally, there'll be a thorough sceptic
Who simply takes his clothes off, and puts none on.

DRIVING

Driving in rush hour traffic
I saw behind the wheel
Of a car hurtling straight at me
The face of my friend Patrick

Who died twenty years ago
Driving in rush hour traffic,
And I was so afraid
To see those eyes that I

Was sure were his fix mine
That for a moment I
Lost all control, and almost
Did as he did years ago.

'DO YOU REMEMBER THOSE FEW HOURS WE SPENT'

Do you remember those few hours we spent
Enchanted by the pictures at the Frick?

Whole rooms – thank God! – abandoned to mere charm,
To versions of *douceur* and dignity

(As if the two of them encompassed all
That might be said of life without a shudder);

And in the atrium the fountain plashing,
The almost silence, and the little frog.

Then, as we stepped outside, the swirling snow.

FLYING BACK

The airport's cluttered lounge presents
The usual mob of miscreants –
The loud, the ugly, and the stupid,
The sad sacks never blessed by Cupid:
But I can't hate the human zoo,
I'll soon be flying back to you.

The conversations swirl around me,
Elsewhere I know they would have drowned me –
But let them prattle, let them chatter,
Nothing they say will ever matter –
I bless the whole loquacious crew,
And think of flying back to you.

The screaming infant, and the bore
Who's got the skinny on the war,
The cell-phone junkie, and the jerk
Who tells me how tax shelters work
I love them all, I really do,
I'm flying back, right now, to you.

And in the plane I'm sat beside
Some fat fanatic Woe-Betide
Who tells me in great detail why

Sinners like me are damned . . . but I
Just nod and murmur 'Whoop-de-do',
Happily flying back to you.

This airline ought to be unlawful,
The flight's delayed, the food is awful,
The stolid stewardess ignores me,
I've brought the wrong book and it bores me –
But I'm not mad or sad or blue . . .
Because I'm flying back to you.

THREE EMILYS

for Emily Grosholz

An adolescent solipsist, I clung to
The law laid down in Haworth parsonage;
I knew the empty uplands you had sung to
And took your tempests as my heritage.
I grew into the world, and came to learn
That one can sing but also think and speak;
Amherst had spoken once, and I would earn
The right to be as accurate and oblique.
Now the world's here; there's nowhere else to go to.
Dear Emily, your gentle words have shown
Here is the truth the winds of childhood blow to,
Its beauty and its horror are our own:
Here is the happiness and grief we grow to,
The shared sweet world, in which we are alone.

TURGENIEV AND FRIENDS

Trained by a brutal father, they became
The divas Malibran and Viardot;
The techniques they had mastered blow by blow
Divided Paris with their florid fame.
Meanwhile, in Oryel, a young mother beat
Her whimpering child to make a man of him;
In time he would become a synonym
For all that's empathetic and discreet.

He fell in love with Viardot, whose spouse
Was understanding, and seemed not to mind;
They lived *à trois*, three mutually kind,
Concerned companions in a single house.
They must have traded stories, but who knows
If their compulsions ever came to blows?

UNDER $6 A BOTTLE

Shun Chardonnay – the bottle might be pretty,
But its bouquet's distinctly eau-de-kitty

Be wary of Bordeaux, which Brits call 'claret' –
Imagine a metallic-tasting carrot

Watch out for anything that fizzes – Asti
Spumante is spectacularly nasty

Avoid Shiraz – there's nothing subtly Persian
About the blatant blowsy Aussie version

Don't risk the Riesling – not, that is, unless you
Know alcoholic Kool-Aid won't distress you

Choose nothing then, put all your icky picks back,
And cross the aisle to buy a Miller six-pack.

'THEY ARE NOT LONG, THE DAYS
OF WINE AND ROSES...'

I think it was the Parthians
Who first homed in on wine and roses
As *sine quibus non* when we
Discuss the good life and its pleasures.

Almost erased by history,
A shadow behind texts, a few
Prosaic ruins, enigmatic
Statues, a derisive catchphrase...

But still, that's quite a legacy.

SHOPPING

Was there a special Mess you had in mind, sir?
If you could be a little more specific...
As you can see we've every size and kind, sir,
From In Your Face to Mildly Soporific.

Adultery is very popular —
It's our perennial favourite, you could say:
The Shocking Pink? Most customers prefer
Discreeter models, like this Sordid Grey.

Self-Poisonings are on sale, and very buyable:
We stock *Old Fogey's Alcoholic Haze,*
The Sixties' Acid Test, and this reliable
La Mode Cocaine; it's ultrachic these days.

Loony obsessions can be quite attractive —
Religious Manias are on that wall,
They come in Solitary or Interactive;
Some say they make the biggest Mess of all.

There's Basic Selfishness, a classic line,
And always guaranteed to stay in style;
I know I couldn't function without mine —
It makes a Mess that's wonderfully worthwhile.

Still not convinced? A canny customer!
I've one more product that might interest you:
This cut-price Boredom is a beauty, sir —
And it'll do what all the others do.

CHAGRIN

In middle age, to my chagrin I find
That death and sex preoccupy my mind.
When de la Mare was gravely ill a kind
Friend asked if there were things for which he pined –
Flowers, say? Or fruit? Politely he declined:
'Too soon for flowers, too late for fruit.' Behind
His wit my past and prospects are defined.

PASTS

The past's quaint versions of the past delight
Our tolerance with gauche anachronisms:
Ovid is *fin amor* plus archaisms,
Swooning Lucretia's stays are laced too tight,
Great Alexander is a Christian knight.
We patronize their pretty solecisms,
And even envy the distorting prisms
That bathed their pasts in such familiar light.

We're too aware to do that now, we say,
Too conscience-stricken, too sophisticated,
Although we know our empathies betray
Our own impedimenta half-translated,
And someone will be tickled pink one day
To come across the pasts that we've created.

A VISIT TO GRANDMOTHER'S

for CT, who told me this story

When shampoo stung her eyes
Her anguished bathroom cries
Of 'Oh' and 'Oooh' and 'Ah'
Were heard by grandmamma
As something else completely.
Later she said, discreetly,
'Lovely to hear your noise:
A young girl who enjoys
Her body won't need boys.'

CAN WE?

Can we convincingly pretend,
And not to others but ourselves,
That we are happy? And if we could,
Would that mean that we were, pro tem,
Uncomplicatedly, just that,
Happy? And what would that be like?
The mind runs through its obvious
Loved carnal candidates... Well, maybe.
But probably it would resemble

Less some celestial debauch
With someone quite phenomenal
Than being in a symphony
By Haydn: having all of it –
It doesn't matter much which one –
The whole ebullient edifice,
Just there, available and real,
Impossibly to hand, forever.

CYTHÈRE

Though we can start with Botticelli –
The blonde hair streaming, and the eyes
Fixed in provocative surprise,
Her hand strategic on her belly –

Your avatars dissolve and morph;
Flesh volatized to soul, the whore
Whose flesh is cash and something more,
Punk wraith, unwieldy Willendorf,

The skinny-dipper at Lake Tahoe,
The floating world, *la belle poitrine*
Of a long-dead Minoan queen,
The plenitude of Khajuraho . . .

But now, for me, you coalesce
As French, immediate, medieval,
Making improbably coeval
Iseut, Watteau, *Bonjour Tristesse*.

I see you now, your body bare
And welcoming, your eyes intense
With passionate intelligence.
Your hands in mine, adored Cythère.

YOUNG SCHOLAR

She puts aside a rival's tome
(*Amor de lonh*, or mythic Rome).

Time for her bath (it's after seven),
And Renée Fleming storming heaven:

She's here to heal: to slough away
The crude detritus of the day.

A sip of wine; the recognition
That what she is is her decision.

Mind makes its peace; the mind's her home.
Cleansed now, she rises from the foam.

FARSIGHTED

Being farsighted means
You can't make out the scenes

Happening before your eyes –
They come as a surprise.

The more remote the view
The more it speaks to you.

And clearly you can't read
That horrid snakelike screed

The world delights to call
The writing on the wall.

ON A REMARK OF KARL KRAUS

('All right, we can sleep together, but no intimacy!')

His paradox
No longer shocks;
It's just a fact now,
The way we act now.

We use, are used,
And disabused
Find coupling hateful.
Karl Kraus, be grateful

For old complexes:
Who says no sex is
The worst or only
Way to be lonely?

'I LAY DOWN IN THE DARKNESS OF MY SOUL'

I lay down in the darkness of my soul
And knew that I was neither sick nor whole,
That lack defined me, and my absent presence
Was not contingent to me, but my essence.

PREFERENCES

    To my surprise
I've come to realize
I don't like poetry

    (Dear, drunkly woozy,
Accommodating floozy
That she's obliged to be,

    Poor girl, these days).
No, what I love and praise
Is not damp poetry

    But her pert, terse,
Accomplished sibling: verse.
She's the right girl for me.

SMALL TALK

Not-Waking

Sleep is the happy lover who
Has no desire to let you go.

'Stay in my arms,' she says, 'Don't move.
Lie still, and be assured of love.'

Imitatio

Our lives are calques of others' lives:
The metaphor is what survives.
Role-play, soothsay, then tell me who
You think you are when you are you.

'Live all you can; it's a mistake not to'

Of course, to recognize
This quote, and more, its truth
Means your myopic youth
Was spent quite otherwise.

Magic

I can imagine someone knowing you,
Turning the pages of the O.E.D.
And carefully cutting out the words that mean
'Goodbye', 'Farewell', so you could never say them,
Then inking over all the words that mean
'Anguish', 'Grief', 'Loss', so he could never see them.

Soteriological

To make another person your salvation
Is to be doubly sure of your damnation.

'Interpretation is the revenge of the intellect upon art'

Dead authors are the easiest to bully,
And few enough will take them at their word:
'We must, if we're to understand X fully...'
X marks the spot where parricide occurred.

Author, Translator...

Author, translator; now their voices switch.
Ventriloquist and doll; but which is which?

Damnation à la Mode

The various martyrdoms' ungodly promises
Ensure damnation to all doubting Thomases.

But let them preach their millenarian premises;
Eros and alcohol remain my nemeses.

Finding

We find that we outgrow, and are outgrown,
And end where we departed from, alone.

There

Absence becomes unbearable: old men
Spell out the scriptures from a distant childhood.
I shall be one of them I know, despite
The incredulity of some I pray for.

Acculturation

'This was our life,' the parents said,
'The moral, only, life – so follow it.'
But long before the fools were dead
They saw the children wouldn't swallow it.

Spleen

How did it happen that life didn't happen,
That nothing turned out the way it was meant to –
That though we set sail for the Fortunate Isles
Cape Disappointment's the landfall we're sent to?

THE PHOENIX

Gold against blue, the fabled phoenix flies,
A mote borne upward by obscure desire –
A sudden signature of lambent fire
Glimpsed for a moment in the spirit's skies.

But look, the cynosure of wondering eyes
Descends and labours, huge now, a machine
That Leonardo might have dreamed he'd seen
Beating its creaking vans through Tuscan skies;

An artifice of grief that cannot rise,
A Hindenburg of hope, whose flagrant crash
We flinch from, breathing Pentecostal ash
As motes swirl upward to uncertain skies.

DIS'S DEFENCE

Now that you've heard the prosecution's case
You think I haven't got a leg to stand on:
'How dare that senile death's-head lay a hand on
Our pretty paragon of youth and grace,
And drag her down to such a dismal place?'
But hold off on the verdict that you've planned on
Until you've heard my side. Let's not abandon
The court's proceedings now, *in medias res*.

Granted, she didn't want to come at first,
But she got used to it, and she's a queen there.
How can you claim my country is 'accursed'
When you admit that none of you has been there?
And every single time I've set her free
Eight months go by, and she comes back to me.

WILLIAM McGONAGALL WELCOMES THE INITIATIVE FOR A GREATER ROLE FOR FAITH-BASED EDUCATION

Oh for the pure Intellectual Fever
Of Halal Madrasseh and Kosher Yeshiva

Where every last pupil's exactly like you
And with only one Answer it *has* to be true

Oh for the play of Disinterested Mind
The impartial inquiry you're certain to find

Where a Catholic Priest can tell you what's what
And ensure that you never encounter a Prot

Where a Protestant Elder can call you to order
And assure you the Pope should be swimming in ordure

Oh for the stirring, sanguinary stories
That admonish us all with Our Martyrs' past glories

Oh for the splendours of Faith-Based Education
That spread Fear and Hatred throughout the whole Nation.

WILLIAM MORRIS

Dyeing Topsy, hands imbrued,
Dreams of scarlet brotherhood:

Pattern pattern all the day
Pattern beareth the bell away.

Dante Gabriel's always there
Painting gentle Janey's hair:

Pattern pattern all the day
Pattern beareth the bell away.

Guinevere needs no defence,
Lovely Janey jumps the fence:

Pattern pattern all the day
Pattern beareth the bell away.

Kelmscott, Iceland, anti-scrape,
Can't undo pandemic rape:

Pattern pattern all the day
Pattern beareth the bell away.

All the fruit is over-ripe,
Dying Topsy sets the type:

Pattern pattern all the day
Pattern beareth the bell away.

DRIVING WESTWARD

The restaurant's full, and I'm a stranger here,
But they accommodate me in a corner.
No wine list. H'm. I order local beer.
The air-conditioning's out. It's like a sauna.

The so-so food's generic U.S.-Thai,
The décor 'Hollywood meets Old Siam' –
Call it the gastronomic *King and I*.
Am I still glad I stopped here? Yes I am.

A mainly student eatery it seems:
Their voices' brief collisions and collusions
Recount the cynicism of their dreams;
'But she's so full of shit!' 'You mean illusions.'

The waitresses are Thai; slim and aloof,
Their slight hauteur's more touching than annoying –
Self-parody perhaps, but vivid proof
That kitsch can comfort us and not be cloying.

'Did you enjoy your meal, sir?' 'It was swell.'
(We're in the Fifties, yes?) The place is thriving.
I tip them far too much. I wish them well:
Replete, content, I can continue driving.

ARE WE GOING THE SAME WAY?

These chance encounters which
      I can't put down to chance
Leave me confused, co-opted
      In someone else's dance.

The e-mails that you send me
      Seem sober, sane, and sensible –
But twice a day's becoming
      A bit, well, indefensible.

The phone rings as I write this
      And answering it I speak
To silence – as I've done
      So many times this week:

That can't be you now, can it?
      You're such a fluent talker;
At least you were before
      You turned into my stalker.

EMBLEMS

Wind-bowed, the peonies' fragility
But also their resilience for a while
Seem emblematic of the lovers' state;

The struggling lovers who negotiate
By stratagems, by honesty, and guile
To be what they obscurely have to be.

A MYSTERY NOVEL

Alone and diffident
You enter what is there:
The world that does not care
For your predicament,

For mysteries of who
You must become, or what
Your place is in the plot
To which you have no clue.

Turn pages; suffer time:
And, look, you are the thread
Unravelling from the dead;
The clue; the plot; the crime.

New Poems

A STORM IN THE MID-WEST

Its mother, choleric as hell, is hurling
Abuse at our poor house. How has it failed
This time? The foam-flecks of her rage go swirling
About the yard; a trash-can has just sailed
Across the driveway, flung wide by her wrath.
And then, as suddenly, the weather clears –
Sunlight is gentle to the trash-strewn path
And dries the windows' iridescent tears.

Where is she now? In heaven with her gin
And lover? Never mind, she has withdrawn.
The sodden garden-cushions are brought in,
The broken branches gathered from the lawn –
As if a child, with careful neatness, could
Deflect her next-time ire by being good.

THE LIGHTHOUSE

When, as a child, I lay alone with dread
I knew the dark could never be complete;
I watched the faithful lighthouse beam repeat
Its passage through my room, across my bed,
As if it were a messenger that said,
  'I'm always here my child, you need not weep,
  Mine is a promise that I'll always keep –
  You need not fear the living or the dead.'

Now there's no beam to interrupt the night
My sleepless vigils are still visited
By greyly shifting shafts of ghostly light
That play upon the wasteland of my bed;
Their transience is the message they repeat –
Only the dark can ever be complete.

A PERSONAL SONNET

How strange this life is mine, and not another,
This jigsaw . . . each irrevocable piece.
That bad, unfinished business of my brother,
Dead at nineteen; my gadding years in Greece
And Italy; life lived, not understood;
A sunset in Kerala, when it seemed
The sun had risen on my life for good.
All this was real, but seems now as if dreamed.

The presences I've loved, and poetry –
Faces I cannot parse or paraphrase
Whose mystery is all that they reveal;
The Persian poets who laid hands on me
And whispered that all poetry is praise:
These are the dreams that turned out to be real.

TO TAKE COURAGE IN CHILDHOOD

The humdrum home becomes a spellbound place
Where life's laid down, indelibly, for good;
This is the meaning of a mother's face,
Here is the garden that is Dante's wood

Where you're to be undone, it seems, forever.
The florid beasts step forward, and the guide
Who whispers, 'This is no time to be clever' –
What horrors will you witness at his side?

Remember though, my child, as you descend
Into the darkness that you're certain hates you
This will not be your home. And in the end
It's Beatrice, not Virgil, who awaits you.

BRAHMS

Young Brahms played piano in a brothel parlour:
He watched the beery patrons go upstairs
And said, 'Non olet', pocketing his thaler,
But something nasty caught him unawares.
He never made it with a girl it seems;
His love was Clara Schumann, who had far
Too much to cope with to indulge his dreams –
Mad Robert flared out like a shooting star.

I couldn't take to Brahms when I was young –
Too sentimental, learnèd, ponderous,
I thought. Now that I find I live among
Such damning adjectives myself, I'm less
Inclined to carp, and if the cap fits wear it;
Let's hear your heartache, Brahms; yes, I can bear it.

A WINTER'S TALE

There was the quarrel and his shrugged-off wife
(Whose hurt heart turned, perhaps, in time to stone) –
The opportunity to shape his life
As he would wish, decisively alone.
There was success, the mountebank who made
The fictions of his inwardness come true,
And there were other loves for which he paid
With loathing for the new self he now knew.

There was regret, the image of a child
That he had lost, that time could not restore;
There was the hunger to be reconciled.
Stratford again – and there, his own front door.
The statue moved and, gently, she descended,
And all the mighty fictions were now ended.

THE MISSING TALE

He was ever (God wot) women's friend
GAVIN DOUGLAS, OF CHAUCER

The women wander in his curious mind;
Their otherness enchants him – duchess, wench,
Exempla earnest moralists maligned,
His wife, whose liquid mother tongue was French
The lingua franca of the nobly born;
Ovid's poor heroines, betrayed Criseyde,
Abandoned Dido angry and forlorn,
The raddled harridan, the pious maid.

That court case, when he was accused of rape,
Who could believe that? Chaucer as abuser?
Real violence? Blackmail? or a silly scrape
Gone wrong? And who was she? My mind pursues her,
Trying to give her allegations shape –
Wanting to hear the tale of his accuser.

TRANSLATING A MEDIEVAL POEM

    How tenderly you lift
The friable, grave-relic from
      The earth where it was found;
     The dust begins to sift
Homeward immediately, drily
     Returning to its ground,

Until what's left is just
A smudge upon your finger ends.
    What is there to display?
        Five fingers touched with dust.
You hold them to the light. 'Come here,
    Look what I've found,' you say.

WIL MILLS (1969–2011)

Once in a speeding car at night, I heard
Your voice sing out, plangent and weirdly strong
In a wailing country *a cappella*,
Yeats's 'He Wishes for the Cloths of Heaven'.

So vigorous and vulnerable the sound,
As if an adolescent angry angel
Were suddenly beside us in the dark,
Defiant and admonishing, afraid.

WALKING THE DOG

We walked our spaniel down
An avenue of trees,
Its lacy architecture
Crisp in the slight breeze –

As if it were a church
And we approached the door,
Though we've been married now
For thirty years and more.

Then drops appeared before us,
Seeding the summer ground;
And in the distance rumbled
Black thunder's sultry sound.

We hoisted my umbrella
And stood beneath a tree,
A pillar in the church
Uniting you and me.

We watched the drops roll down,
Then pour, then pelt and splash
Our sodden happy dog.
And now the thunder's crash

Seemed over us; 'You're soaked,'
I said, 'don't catch a chill –
The storm's not letting up;
Come closer . . . closer still.'

THE FALL

I felt your sleeping body jerk and sprawl
        Alive with terror...
They say our treetop ancestors might fall
        In fatal error

Down to the forest floor where who knows what
        Monsters might claim us,
And fears the long millennia forgot
        Still nightly maim us.

Is this then why salvation always meant
        For us a rising
Into the blue sustaining firmament...
        Is that surprising?

And that last spasm of our being, will
        It be the fall,
Or the imagined leap to heaven's sill
        Redeeming all?

Don't be ridiculous, your body says,
        Settling in sleep...
Darkness is ours, the treetop soughs and sways,
        Your dreams are deep.

FOR MY MOTHER-IN-LAW, DURING HER LAST ILLNESS

How much estranges us –
Gender and generation,
The incivilities
That nation speaks to nation,
Parochial workings out
Of custom, cult, belief;
Even what can be thought
Appropriate in grief.

How much though draws me to
Your side now in my mind,
Wanting to honour you,
Remembering the kind
Uncomplicated way
You said my future wife
Should have at least some say
In how she'd spend her life.

Your husband's angry fiat
Forbidding us to wed
Became at last 'So be it'
Softened by all you'd said;
I owe my happiness
To your persistent voice
Suggesting 'No' or 'Yes'
Should be your daughter's choice.

I see your modest gaze,
Your gestures and your smile,
The self-effacing ways
Your goodness would beguile

Those who were with you to —
Inexplicably — find
Themselves as blessed as you,
As resolutely kind.

A DREAM

That image of my mother, beautiful
As I had never known her, chic and slim,
In clothes she could have owned when I was born,
Her waist tight-cinched, her neat chapeau so jaunty,
Her young face full of tipsy happiness,
Whence did it come? And whence too came the light
From which she gazed at me, beyond all judgment,
As if we shared some silent understanding?
This was a memory I never had,
But even so my dream insisted on it.

NEW DEVELOPMENT

The swing-sets rhyming in the tidy yards,
The prepubescent girls in leotards,
The saplings not yet sure that they are here
Still learning how the seasons shape the year,
The puppies gambolling, snapping, feigning fights
That end with nuzzles and pretended bites.

O summer afternoons of innocence,
O wholesome industry, sweet indolence,
Where propped-up dolls sit seriously around
A tiny tea-set on the grassy ground,
As if their earnest play could substitute
Forever for worlds crueller and less cute.

DARWINIAN

Sorrow is ineluctable, not just
Among ourselves. The doctor he was meant
To be could never mitigate so much,
The stunted children in the factories,
The famished street-walker, the beggar who
Was turned away with nothing from our doors.
Within those doors the bullied and abandoned,
The beaten child who cries himself to sleep
And is afraid to wake.

                 He felt them all
Connected to him by an endless skein
Clogging him like the gossamer of ropes
With which the swarming Lilliputians held
Poor Gulliver, who had to get away.
The Beagle proved to be the quiet place,
His sober, meditative sanctuary;
But even so they had to put ashore.
The great man grew indignant at the plight
Of slaves and fulminated in his letters,
Excoriating Christendom so-called
That could so blithely countenance such cruelty.

And then there was the world of animals.
Just how far down life's ramifying tree
Did all this go (the mourning elephant,
Pack animals who drive the weakest out,
His terrier, and the earthworms whom he tested
To see if they were sensitive to sound . . .)?
So that at times all life could seem to be
A panoply of never-ending grief,
Immense, implacable, and everywhere.

Strange how this man of tortured empathy
So boundless it encompassed all the earth
Should have his name usurped by social schemes
Of conscious callousness and willed indifference.

THE MAPLE TREE

The maple tree beyond my window lifts
Its limbs with an exuberance of being,
In spring at least. In winter something shifts
And when I glance up what I think I'm seeing
Is now a dark, contorted agony –
A Laocoön inwardness of pain
Alive in knots and burls, a tragedy
Of guilt and grief made intimately plain.

And not a jot of this is true of course.
My maple tree, and all its like, proceed
Oblivious of happiness, remorse,

And every other human sense or need.
We give to them what only we possess
As if this might assuage our loneliness.

THE INTRODUCTION

Autobiography's not something I
Have felt in any way impelled to try,
But since, whenever people reminisce
About romantic moments – their first kiss,
The flowers he sent, the perfume of her hair –
And my turn comes, and they hear when and where
I met my wife, someone will always say,
'You really ought to write that down one day',
Here goes...

                It was in 1971,
My new job in Tehran had just begun,
And I fell sick. I saw a doctor who
Said there was not much wrong, and in her view
Brisk walks and whisky would take care of it
(This hale-and-hearty was an ex-pat Brit).
I did as I was told, and found that I
Got sicker still, and rather thought I'd die.
A friend discovered me, passed out, in bed;
She, when she'd ascertained I wasn't dead,
Summoned a much more competent MD
(Iranian this time), who immediately
Dispatched me in the speeding ambulance
That carried me, unconscious, to romance.

The nurse whose job was to admit me checked
My vital signs; her hand could not detect
Much pulse at all, beyond a feeble flicker,
And I was clearly, quickly, getting sicker.
The doctors were all busy. What to do?
She had them paged, but no one came; she knew,
Or thought she knew, that doing nothing would
Ensure the flicker would go out for good.
And then, despite awareness of the fact
That breaking rules like this could get her sacked,
She did the cross-match pronto, and proceeded
To give me the transfusion that I needed.

When I came round at last the doctor said,
'We very nearly gave you up for dead;
This nurse, Ms. Darbandi here, saved your life.'
This was my introduction to my wife.

WINE

for Afkham, of course

When we were young, and poorer, we made wine;
The elderberry was like vinegar,
But it was easy, and the colour seemed
An emblem of the elemental joy
We often shared in those still heady days;
It was a funny standby, not a failure
(Unlike the really foul potato which
Not even we could bring ourselves to drink).
The humble parsnip made a potent brew
That looked like cow-piss but passed muster once
You let it talk to you, and knocked you out
If you weren't careful to go easy on it.

Our triumph was the elderflower, that took
What seemed a world of careful preparation –
Catching the blossoms on the perfect day,
Getting the sugar that we added right,
And even then it seemed more chancy than
The less exalted bottles that were crammed
Against it in the dark beneath our staircase.
But when it worked it was our shared champagne,
As light and giggly as a secret joke,
As heart-bewitching as a pilfered kiss.

And now, whatever wines I pour (Vouvray,
Champagne's champagne, Barolo, two buck chuck),
The first sip still remains a silent toast
To what, for me, a drawn cork always conjures:
The taste of happiness, from long ago.

ADMONITION FOR THE SEVENTH DECADE

All the bluster and conceit,
All the hare-brained indiscreet
Obfuscations and obsessions,
All the ludicrous confessions,
Put them by now, put them by,
Clean them out before you die.

Even though you can't undo
All the mess that makes up you,
Find a modicum of quiet;
Quash the long uncivil riot
That goes on inside your heart;
Clear the drunks out, make a start.

CAMPANILISMO

When I was a child and still at school
I was told to sit up, not to play the fool,
And to realize ('Are you listening, Davis?')
That Shakespeare is Poetry's *rara avis*,
The best of all, the *ne plus ultra*,
The utter acme of all culture.

And when much later I went to Greece
A drunk Greek told me the Golden Fleece,
The phoenix of verse, is clearly Homer,
Everyone else is a mere misnomer –

No, Homer is best, the *ne plus ultra*,
The utter acme of all culture.

And Yes when I worked in Italy
An assertive Italian lectured me
On poets and verse, and upped the ante
By strenuously supporting Dante
As best of all, the *ne plus ultra*,
The utter acme of all culture.

I went to Iran – you've guessed the rest,
It was Hafez this time who was the best,
The Unseen's Tongue, Guide to the Hidden,
The rose on history's stinking midden –
Greatest of all, the *ne plus ultra*,
The utter acme of all culture.

In the USA, the much maligned,
They tend to be less wilfully blind;
They've shit to peddle but not that shit, man –
No one puts forth the claims of Whitman
As best of all, the *ne plus ultra*,
The utter acme of all culture.

LATER

If you hear Haydn somewhere, I won't say
'Remember me.' But, it could be, that you,
As his benign configurations play,
Might briefly think, 'Perhaps Dick hears this too.'

And if you're struck by beauty in a verse
And shiver then, as if the room grew colder,
And blink back irksome tears, you could do worse
Than think I read there too, behind your shoulder.

So, when red wine is poured, and candles cast
Ambiguous glamour on each glance and smile,
Invite me, if you wish to, from the past
To drink, and share your laughter for a while.

KEEPING A DIARY

Whoever's fumbled, flattered, wed, or dead,
Pepys writes, to end the day, 'And so to bed.'

And since whatever happens, sweet or grim,
These days I end the day by reading him,

Before my book drops and my body sleeps,
My sign-off phrase is now, 'And so to Pepys.'

EURO-TRASH

How is it that an opera has to sound
(The pitch and tempi, all the instruments,
The coloratura's fiddly ornaments)
As close as possible to what we might
Have heard on its now long-ago first night –

While any notion that it ought to look
Like something we'd have seen as well as heard
On that same night is treated as absurd
By self-important idiots hell-bent
On being cutting-edge and relevant?

Why must the sounds be right when all along
The sights we see are so grotesquely wrong?

PAYING FOR IT

You put your questions to the world. She hears,
Behind your eloquence, your abject fears:

'Tell me if I am loved. Can anyone,
Can you, undo the evil that I've done?'

She smiles, and takes your clothes off as you speak.
'Naked', in any language, equals 'weak'.

This is her job. She looks you in the eye.
She says, 'You're wonderful. I'm yours. Don't cry.'

There, you believe her, don't you? Though you know
That when she indicates you have to go

The grubby notes you leave upon the shelf
Are IOUs for what you call your self.

THE SAVING GRACE

for Sai Bhatawadekar, who pointed this out to me

Dreaming of truth and heaven
And heavenly retribution,
Remember grammar's humble
Decisive contribution;

Remember Goethe's Faust
Who, facing sure damnation,
Chose the subjunctive mood
And so achieved salvation.

GOING, GOING...

Urquhart and Aretino got it right
When facing the unknowable hereafter?
No piety was there, no funk of fright,
Only a fit of apoplectic laughter.

RECONNOITRING

Slowly, with caution, then with quickening joy,
The dogs' tails wag as girl approaches boy;

Their noses sniff each other, and then dart
Downward to get at the important part.

Their doggy groins are severally explored;
An act that's simultaneously ignored

And seen by both the owners, who now chat
With courteous bonhomie on this and that,

Assessing underneath their cautious greetings
The possibilities of further meetings.

LEAVING THE FAIR

Imagine that you're at a raucous fair,
The kind you went to sixty years ago –
The beckoning booths, just pennies for a throw,
Loud barkers, louder hawkers everywhere,
Such promises of pleasure in the air . . .
A plunging carousel, a puppet show,
A tent for movies, Marilyn Monroe
Fixing the tumult with her glaucous stare.

And now you walk away from all its noise,
The too bright colours busy in your mind
But less so since you're leaving them behind
As if you knew they're someone else's toys.
That's what old age is like . . . the whole shebang
An echo of a song a stranger sang.

TO VIS

On translating Gorgani's Vis and Ramin

I came to you, how many years ago,
      And felt the stirrings of
A puzzled sympathy I could not know
      Would turn, in time, to love;
Love that took on the idiom you taught
      The foreign heart you'd caught.

And how insistently you chivvied me . . .
      'When will you get to work?'
'A little time, Vis, give me time, you'll see.'
      'Dick, all you do is shirk
Your promises . . . Why do you make them then?
      You're weak, like other men!'

And so I sat, before day dawned, each day
      And parsed your words, and turned
To English rhymes the words you'd have me say.
      And page by page I learned
The life I gave was yours alone to give,
      And yours the life I live.

A STUDENT READING *VIS AND RAMIN*

Some slowly, some with sudden confidence,
She says the Persian words — her serious face
Ambushed by pleasure as she grasps the sense
Of love a thousand years could not efface.

She looks up then, and in her glance I see
How eagerly she reaches to embrace
The wraiths of realization, empathy . . .
Pleasures a thousand years will not efface.

TRANSLATING HAFEZ, OR TRYING TO

How long you've teased me with your tropes, Hafez,
And led me on, and dashed my hopes, Hafez,

And left me like a foolish fog-bound man
Who pats and peers and grasps and gropes, Hafez,

And thinks he's getting somewhere till he takes
A tumble down delusion's slopes, Hafez,

And nursing angry broken bones declares,
'God damn the guide, god damn the ropes, Hafez.'

Your imperturbability is like
A really irritating pope's, Hafez –

All wealth that's poverty, and wine that's not,
And metaphoric cloaks and copes, Hafez . . .

But there, no matter how much Dick complains
Or goes off in a sulk, or mopes, Hafez,

Tomorrow finds him shaking (just once more)
Your glittering kaleidoscopes, Hafez.

WWHD?

for Alicia Stallings

He lived, like most men, during times that seemed
Especially intractable, and wrote
    His poems accordingly.

His king said that his poems' lines appeared
To be quite unaware of one another;
    His answer's not recorded.

He liked to pun on words to do with wine
And music, to use tropes a tyro'd label
    Unmanageably tricky.

His hatreds were hypocrisy, and minds
That claimed exclusive access anywhere;
    Compassion was his bailiwick

And kindred souls his notion of the good-life.
You could do worse in crises than to ask,
    'So, What Would Hafez Do'?

WORDS

Words are like scree – abraded, hard, but not
At all reliable for climbing on;
Just look how far you've slipped back, trusting them.

Selected Translations

NOTE ON THE TRANSLATIONS

The translations included here are from Persian, and are taken from the following books: *The Conference of the Birds* (1984), *Borrowed Ware: Medieval Persian Epigrams* (1996, 1997), *The Shahnameh: the Persian Book of Kings* (2006, 2007, 2016), *Vis and Ramin* (2008, 2009), *Faces of Love: Hafez and the Poets of Shiraz* (2012, 2013). The poets whose work is represented in the following pages lived during the medieval period, the earliest in the 10th century, the latest in the 14th. In order to give some notion of what reading these poems in Persian is like, I have tried in making these translations to keep as closely as I could to the Persian forms, as their formal elements constitute a large part of their effect. For example, all Persian narrative poems are in couplets, and I have translated them into couplets in English; the lyric forms are more complicated and harder to bring off in English, but again I have tried to reproduce, as far as I could, at least some formal effects of the originals. The extracts from *The Conference of the Birds* were translated in conjunction with my wife, Afkham Darbandi; I must take sole responsibility for the other translations here, although Afkham often made suggestions when I consulted her about tricky or ambiguous moments, and I almost always accepted them.

From Farid ud-din Attar's *The Conference of the Birds*, mid 13th century

Farid ud-din Attar's *The Conference of the Birds* is one of the best-known Sufi (mystical) poems in Persian. The poem is an allegory of the mystic quest in which the birds of the world, representing human souls, journey to find their king, the mythical Simorgh. The birds are led by the hoopoe, who functions as their spiritual guide, and tells them anecdotes and tales to describe the way and to encourage them along it. The birds traverse seven valleys, denoting stages of the mystical journey; these are, The Quest, Love, Insight, Detachment, Unity, Bewilderment, and the last, Poverty and Nothingness. Here is the description of the last valley, together with one of the anecdotes the hoopoe tells his avian audience in order to explain its nature.

The Valley of Poverty and Nothingness

Next comes that valley words cannot express,
The Vale of Poverty and Nothingness:
Here you are lame and deaf, the mind has gone,
You enter an obscure oblivion.
When sunlight penetrates the atmosphere
A hundred thousand shadows disappear,
And when the sea arises what can save
The patterns on the surface of each wave?
The two worlds are those patterns, and in vain
Men tell themselves what passes will remain.
Whoever sinks within this sea is blessed
And in self-loss obtains eternal rest;
The heart that would be lost in this wide sea
Disperses in profound tranquillity,
And if it should emerge again it knows
The secret ways in which the world arose.

The pilgrim who has grown wise in the Quest,
The Sufi who has weathered every test,
Are lost when they approach this painful place,
And other men leave not a single trace.
Because all disappear you might believe
That all are equal (just as you perceive
That twigs and incense offered to a flame
Both turn to powdered ash and look the same).
But though they seem to share a common state
Their inward essences are separate,
And evil souls sunk in this mighty sea
Retain unchanged their base identity;
But if a pure soul sinks, the waves surround
His fading form, in beauty he is drowned –
He is not yet he is; what could this mean?
It is a state the mind has never seen . . .

The Moths and the Flame

Moths gathered in a fluttering throng one night
To learn the truth about the candle's light,
And they decided one of them should go
To gather news of the elusive glow.
One flew till in the distance he discerned
A palace window where a candle burned –
And went no nearer; back again he flew
To tell the others what he thought he knew.
The mentor of the moths dismissed his claim
Remarking, 'He knows nothing of the flame.'
A moth more eager than the one before
Set out and passed beyond the palace door.
He hovered in the aura of the fire
A trembling blur of timorous desire,
Then headed back to say how far he'd been
And how much he had undergone and seen.

The mentor said, 'You do not bear the signs
Of one who's fathomed how the candle shines.'
Another moth flew out — his dizzy flight
Turned to an ardent wooing of the light;
He dipped and soared, and in his frenzied trance
Both Self and fire were mingled by his dance —
The flame engulfed his wing-tips, body, head,
His being glowed a fierce translucent red;
And when the mentor saw that sudden blaze,
The moth's form lost within the glowing rays,
He said, 'He knows, he knows the truth we seek,
That hidden truth of which we cannot speak.'
To go beyond all knowledge is to find
That comprehension which eludes the mind,
And you can never gain the longed for goal
Until you first outsoar both flesh and soul;
But should one part of you remain, a single hair
Will drag you back and plunge you in despair —
No creature's Self can be admitted here,
Where all identity must disappear.

From *Borrowed Ware: Medieval Persian Epigrams*

Mahsati and Ayesheh Samarqandi are women poets; the rest are men.

I'll hide within my poems as I write them
Hoping to kiss your lips as you recite them

Amareh, 10th–11th centuries

The deer pursues its doe; a lover searches
    Through the orchard, hoping his belovèd's there:
Grief-stricken, come – bring wine again that frees you
    From this harsh world and all its carking care:
A wind has risen in the flowering willow
    Scattering its blossoms on the drinkers' hair.

Amareh

    Who came to me? She did. And when? At dawn.
Afraid of whom? An enemy. Who is . . .? Her father.
    I kissed her twice. Where? On the lips. The lips?
Say rubies rather. And they were? As sweet as sugar.

Onsori, 11th century

If I could choose to come, I'd not have come;
If I could choose to go, when would I go?
The best would be if I had never come,
And were not here, and did not have to go.

Sana'i, 11th–12th centuries

I always knew – it was as clear as day my love –
That sooner, later, you would go away, my love,
Because when you decided you must leave, my love,
Not even iron chains could make you stay, my love.

Ma'sud Sa'd, 11th century

All day, my heart, you've been upset,
And you, my eyes, are always wet –
But Patience (yesterday you talked
So big!) you haven't turned up yet.

Ashhari, 12th century

Each night, as I was travelling, in each place,
I saw till dawn's first light your haunting face –
But you had sent me Wakefulness for fear
That in my dreams of you we might embrace.

Atai Razi, 11th–12th centuries

In response to a rival poet who said his poems 'lacked salt'

To Ama'q

You say my verse lacks salt – perhaps it's true,
My verse is sweet as sugarcane and honey
And salt should not be added to these two.
Look, pimp – salt's good for beans and turnip stew,
The kind of muck served up as verse by you.

Rashidi, 12th century

A Stingy Patron

Take what he gives you, even if it's paltry –
From this lord *paltry*'s quite a bit;
A gift from him's like being circumcised –
Once in a lifetime, and that's it!

Anvari, 12th century

I wrote a panegyric on you – and I'm sorry.
    There's no point in these lays of one's own making;
My praise was like a wet dream – when I woke I found
    I'd spent spunk on a worthless undertaking.

Anvari

Me, three other poets, six tailors, and four clerks
Were captured by two horsemen – it was infamous . . .
But poets, clerks, and tailors can't put up a fight –
Not if there are fourteen – or four thousand – of us!

Anvari

The one your beauty's overthrown
        has come back home
The one who thirsts for you alone
        has come back home;
Prepare the cage again, scatter your seeds
        of kindness there,
Look, broken-winged, the bird you own,
        has come back home.

Mahsati, 12th century

You're no great intellect, and men like you don't know
The usual kindnesses a lover ought to show –
My flighty friend, I'm glad I'm with you here tonight,
I hope I don't regret it in the morning though . . .

Mahsati

Glimpsing your lovely face, my poor eyes stare
And brim with water like spring clouds; but there –
You are the sun; the eyes of anyone
Will water if he gazes at the sun.

Tajaddin Bakharzi, 12th century

To learn, you need a teacher – one who knows.
You think that books alone will do the trick?
You're like a hen untrodden by the rooster –
Nice eggs, but they won't hatch a single chick.

Shatranji, 12th century

However often I give up on love
And live again with Health and Common Sense,
Some pretty face will pass me by and then
Lunacy makes short work of Abstinence.

Sefaddin Bakharzi, 12th–13th centuries

My hated love, last night and all night too,
They, curse them, told me stories about you –
Their gossip was you break your promises;
And d'you know what? – my heart said, 'Yes, it's true.'

Ayesheh Samarqandi, 13th century

If you should say to me, 'Don't mention love'
I'll manage to restrain my tongue by force,
But if you try prohibiting my tears
The Tigris can't be altered in its course.

Sa'di, 13th century

Until you can correct and heal yourself
Be quiet about another man's disgrace –
Don't be the bare-arsed bullying constable
Who hits a whore and tells her, 'Veil your face!'

Sa'di

Those close to Him make little of the fact,
His is a name they almost never mention;
The windy ones who screech like fifes live far
From Him; that's why they're screeching, for attention.

Afzaladdin, 13th century

The nights I spend with you, love will not let me sleep,
The nights I lie alone, I lie awake and weep;
With you or without you God knows I stay awake—
But look what different forms a sleepless night can take!

Rumi, 13th century

To talk to you about my heart's distress,
                        O God can this be me?
And then to kiss your agate lips no less,
                        O God can this be me?
For me to glimpse you, even from afar,
                        was once impossible –
To sleep with you, to know such happiness
                        O God can this be me?

Sadr-e Zanjani, 13th century

There never was much hope for me with you –
The way you used to be could hardly last;
I knew you'd break the promises you gave,
But not that you would break them quite so fast.

Khosrow Dehlavi, 13th–14th centuries

    To profit from this world and from religion
Know that the heart of both is man's benevolence,
    To seek the rights and comfort of the poor
Will equal any self-denying ordinance –
    And if there is a key to Heaven's gate
It's kindness, and a lack of all malevolence.

Ebn Yamin, 13th–14th centuries

The world's a scale where men are weighed –
The worse they are the more they boast;
But that's the way that scales are made –
The emptier pan's the uppermost.

Anonymous, before 1330

From Ferdowsi's *Shahnameh: the Persian Book of Kings*, completed in 1010

The *Shahnameh* tells the epic history of Iran from the creation of the world until the Arab conquest of the 7th century C.E. The early sections of the poem consist of mythological and legendary stories, the closing sections are quasi-historical. The great hero of the legendary portion of the poem is Rostam, and one of the most famous narratives associated with his name is the tale of Rostam and his son Sohrab, from which the three following extracts are taken.

Rostam has been hunting in a border area and has lost his horse, Rakhsh; he believes Rakhsh has been stolen by warriors from the town of Samangan, so he goes to the town on foot, and demands that his horse be returned to him. He is entertained by the local king, and after an evening of feasting and drinking he is shown to a private room where he can sleep. He wakes to see a young woman standing by his bed; he asks her who she is and she replies:

'My name is Tahmineh; longing has torn
My wretched life in two, though I was born
The daughter of the king of Samangan,
And am descended from a warrior clan.
But like a legend I have heard the story
Of your heroic battles and your glory,
Of how you have no fear, and face alone
Dragons and demons and the dark unknown,
Of how you sneak into Turan at night
And prowl the borders to provoke a fight,
Of how, when warriors see your mace, they quail
And feel their lion hearts within them fail.
I bit my lip to hear such talk, and knew
I longed to see you, to catch sight of you,

To glimpse your martial chest and mighty face –
And now God brings you to this lowly place.
If you desire me, I am yours, and none
Shall see or hear of me from this day on;
Desire destroys my mind, I long to bear
Within my woman's womb your son and heir,
I promise you your horse if you agree
Since all of Samangan must yield to me.'

Tahmineh becomes pregnant from this encounter, and gives birth to a son, Sohrab, who grows up in Turan (central Asia, Iran's enemy throughout the legendary portion of the Shahnameh*). When he is a young man Sohrab leads the forces of Turan against Iran, hoping that he will be able to find his father and set him on the Iranian throne. Sohrab and Rostam meet on the battlefield and each is unaware of who his opponent is, but Sohrab suspects that the old warrior he is facing might be Rostam. However Rostam denies this, since he is afraid that if it is known who he is and he is killed, the army of Turan will be aware that Iran has lost its most formidable warrior and will not hesitate to attack in force and overrun the country. Before they fight Sohrab taunts Rostam with his age, saying that he will be no match for a young man like himself. Rostam replies:*

'So headstrong and so young! Warm words, and bold!
The ground, young warrior, is both hard and cold.
Yes, I am old, and I've seen many wars,
And laid low many mighty conquerors;
Many a demon's perished by my hand
And I've not known defeat, in any land.
Look on me well; if you escape from me
You need not fear the monsters of the sea;
The sea and mountains know what I have wrought
Against Turan, how nobly I have fought,
The stars are witness to my chivalry,
In all the world there's none can equal me.'
Then Sohrab said, 'I'm going to question you,
Your answer must be honest, straight, and true:

I think that you're Rostam, and from the clan
Of warlike Sam and noble Nariman.'
Rostam replied, 'I'm not Rostam, I claim
No kinship with that clan or noble name:
Rostam's a champion, I'm a slave – I own
No royal wealth or crown or kingly throne.'
And Sohrab's hopes were changed then to despair,
Darkening before his gaze the sunlit air.

The two fight; Rostam mortally wounds Sohrab, and as the young man dies he reveals just who it is whom Rostam has killed.

'I brought this on myself, this is from me,
And Fate has merely handed you the key
To my brief life: not you but heaven's vault –
Which raised me and then killed me – is at fault.
Love for my father led me here to die.
My mother gave me signs to know him by,
And you could be a fish within the sea,
Or pitch black, lost in night's obscurity,
Or be a star in heaven's endless space,
Or vanish from the earth and leave no trace,
But still my father, when he knows I'm dead
Will bring down condign vengeance on your head.
One from this noble band will take this sign
To Rostam's hands, and tell him it was mine,
And say I sought him always, far and wide,
And that, at last, in seeking him, I died.'

From Fakhraddin Gorgani's *Vis and Ramin*, mid-11th century

Vis and Ramin is the first major Persian verse romance; the poem is an 11th-century reworking of what was originally a Parthian tale from around the time of Christ, and Gorgani retains many of its pre-Islamic details. It is in several ways an anomalous poem in Persian, since the love between the two main characters is never, as became usual with later writers of romances, spiritualized or given a Sufi/mystical interpretation, but is treated entirely for its secular and physical self. The poem is also unusual in the way that its main characters are virtually all women, and its heroine, Vis (pronounced to rhyme with 'peace'), is perhaps the most strikingly memorable woman in the whole of medieval Persian literature. The story is a love triangle. Vis is promised as a bride to a king before she is even born, and she is married off to him against her will; she and the king's younger brother fall in love and embark on a long adulterous affair. The story is extremely similar in many respects to the European tale of Tristan and Isolde, which it precedes by over a century, and it may well be a major source for this story (for interested readers, the evidence for this is set out in the introduction to the complete translation, from which the following excerpts are taken.)

Vis has been married to her brother Viru (brother-sister marriages were common in the royal and aristocratic families of pre-Islamic Iran, as they were in ancient Egypt; many of the pharaohs were married to their sisters), but is then snatched from Viru and married off to King Mobad. She has not actually slept with either of her husbands as yet, since she and Viru were parted before the marriage could be consummated, and she has persuaded her nurse to put a spell on Mobad that has rendered him impotent with her. Mobad's younger brother Ramin (pronounced to rhyme with 'seen', with the stress on the second syllable) has fallen in love with Vis while escorting her to Mobad's castle, and he uses Vis's nurse as a go-between to persuade Vis to meet him. This takes quite a while, as Vis is reluctant to break her marriage vows despite her intense dislike of her husband:

Now when the nurse saw Vis's furious face
And heard her talk of heaven and God's grace
She searched within her scheming heart to find
Some means to soothe her charge's troubled mind:
Her demon did not rest, but wondered how
Vis and Ramin could be united now,
And how like fat and sugar they could be
Blended entirely, and inseparably.

Then one by one the sly nurse recollected
All the old tricks and spells that she'd collected,
And when she spoke her voice was lovelier than
The frescoes at Noshad.[1] The nurse began:
'You're dearer to me than my soul, more blessed
And virtuous even than I'd ever guessed;
May you seek justice always, may you stay
Truthful and honoured, wise in every way.
Why should I need or want, dear Vis, to grieve you?
What fear or greed could drive me to deceive you?
Why should I want to trick you? I'm not trying
To steal from you, why should I think of lying?
Ramin is not my brother or my son;
And can you tell me what it is he's done
To make me favour him, so that I'd be
His faithful friend and your sworn enemy?
I only want one thing from life, that you
Find happiness in everything you do,
And that your reputation stay intact.
But I must tell you an undoubted fact:
You are a woman, not a demon, not
A fairy, houri, or I don't know what.
Viru has gone, and as for Mobad, well
He's been disposed of by a clever spell:

---

1. Noshad was a legendary pre-Islamic palace of great beauty.

No one's enjoyed your body, no one can,
You've never truly slept with any man.
You've had no joy of men, you've never known
A man whom you could really call your own.
You've married twice, but each time you've moved on;
Both husbands crossed the river, and they're gone!
But if you want a man, I've never seen
A finer specimen than this Ramin:
What use is beauty if it doesn't bless
Your life with pleasure and love's happiness?
You're innocent, you're in the dark about it,
You don't know how forlorn life is without it.
Women were made for men, dear Vis, and you
Are not exempt, whatever you might do.
 The well-born women of the world delight
In marrying a courtier or a knight,
And some, who have a husband, also see
A special friend who's sworn to secrecy;
She loves her husband, she embraces him,
And then her happy friend replaces him.
You can have royal riches beyond measure,
Brocades, and jewels, and every kind of treasure,
But joy is something that you won't discover
Until you have a husband or a lover.
If you need riches it's to make you more
Attractive to him than you were before;
What use are all your red and yellow dresses
Unless they lead to kisses and caresses?
If you can see this, it was wrong of you
To slander me when all I said is true;
I spoke maternally, and as your nurse,
I'm trying to make things better now, not worse.
Ramin is worthy of you, and I've seen
That you, dear Vis, are worthy of Ramin:
You are the sun and he's the moon; if he
Is like an elegant, tall cypress tree,

You are a bough of blossoms in the spring;
If you are milk, he's wine. In everything
You're worthy of each other's love, and I
Will never grieve again until I die
If I can see love mutually requited
When you and he are happily united.'

   And as the nurse spoke, at her voice's sound,
A horde of hellish demons crowded round,
And set a thousand traps, a thousand snares
Before her feet, to catch Vis unawares.
The nurse went on: 'A noble woman spends
Her life in pleasure, with her special friends
Or with her husband; you sit here and sigh,
And weep your heart away, and moan and cry.
Your youth will soon be gone, and you'll have had
No time at all when you were young and glad;
How long will you stay grieving and alone?
You're not composed of brass, my dear, or stone . . .

. . .You're not a God or angel, you are clay,
Like all of us whose lives must pass away,
Desire and longing live in us, and you
Are not exempt, you feel their vigour too.
God made us so that nothing's lovelier than
What we as women feel when with a man,
And you don't know how vehemently sweet
The pleasure is when men and women meet;
If you make love just once, I know that then
You won't hold back from doing so again.'

Vis and Ramin finally meet and swear eternal love to one another:

Vis and Ramin then swore no force could sever
The love that bound the two of them forever.
Ramin spoke first: 'I swear by God, and by
His sovereignty that rules the earth and sky,

I swear now by the sun, and by the light
The shining moon bestows on us at night,
I swear by Venus and by noble Jupiter,
I swear by bread and salt and flickering fire,
I swear by faith and God's omnipotence,
And by the soul and all its eloquence,
That while winds scour the wastelands and the mountains,
While waters flow in rivers and in fountains,
While night has darkness, and while streams have fishes,
While stars have courses, and while souls have wishes,
Ramin will not regret his love, or break
The binding oath that he and Vis now make;
He'll never take another love, or cease
To give his heart exclusively to Vis.'

Vis promised love when Prince Ramin had spoken
And swore her promises would not be broken.
She gave him violets then and murmured, 'Take
This pretty posy, keep it for my sake,
Keep it forever, so that when you see
Fresh violets blooming you'll remember me;
And may the soul that breaks this solemn vow
Darken and droop as these poor flowers do now.
Each time I see the spring's new flowers appear
I will recall the oaths we swore to here;
May anyone that breaks this oath decay
And wither as fresh flowers do – in a day.'

And once these promises of love were given,
And they had called to witness God and heaven,
They lay beside each other telling tales
Of all their former sorrows and travails.
Vis lay beside her prince now, face to face,
The full moon lay in Prince Ramin's embrace,
And when Ramin affectionately placed
His gentle arm about her yielding waist

It was as if a golden torque should grasp
A silver cypress in its circling clasp,
And then Rezvan[2] himself could not declare
Which was the lovelier of this noble pair.
Their pillow smelt of musk, and jewelled bed-covers
Bestrewed with roses lay upon the lovers.
Now lip to lip and cheek to cheek they lay
And struck the ball of pleasure into play;[3]
So close together were their bodies pressed
That rain could not have reached to either's breast,
And Vis's heart was now a balm that cured
The agonies Ramin's heart had endured,
For every wound she'd dealt his heart before
He kissed her face a thousand times and more.

Because their love seems hopeless, Ramin abandons Vis for a while, and in an effort to forget her marries another princess named Gol (which means 'Rose'). Vis writes him a long letter of passionate reproach, in ten sections. Here is the opening of her letter:

From an uprooted, fire-scorched cypress tree
To one that flourishes, alive and free,
From an eclipsed and ever darkened moon
To one that shines now like the sun at noon,
From a poor garden plot where nothing grows
To one where springtime's sweetest blossom blows,
From an emaciated, withered bough
To one whose fruit's the starlit heavens now,
From an abandoned, worked-out, empty mine
To one where all the world's jewels seem to shine,
From one whose western daylight's almost done
To one who greets the newly risen sun,

---

2. Rezvan: the angel who guards the houris of the Islamic paradise, and is thus a connoisseur of beauty.
3. The metaphor is from polo.

From one whose ruby's been plucked out, cast down,
To one whose ruby's set within a crown,
From one whose flowers the dusty wind's destroyed
To one whose flowers are cherished and enjoyed,
From one whose pearl-less sea has shrunk and dried
To one whose pearl-filled sea's a flowing tide,
From one whose darkened fortune's stream is salt
To one whose fortune's sun the heavens exalt,
From one whose feverish love's grown overbold
To one whose love was warm, and has grown cold,
From one whose anguished soul endures distress
To one whose soul knows luck and happiness,
From one whose sight is clouded with disgrace
To one whose glory radiates from his face,
From one who's like worn cloth whose colours fade,
To one who's like a sumptuous brocade,
From eyes that never sleep and always weep,
To eyes that never weep and sweetly sleep,
From kindness, from a faithful, constant friend,
To callous treachery that has no end,
From the sad moon who's lovelorn and alone
To the world's king in splendour on his throne
I write this letter now, so sick at heart
I pray my flesh may die, my soul depart.
 I melt within the flames of separation
While your life's one continuous celebration,
I guard the treasures of fidelity,
While you're oppression's evil deputy.
Now, in this letter, I would have you swear,
By friendship, love, and all we used to share,
By every secret whispered confidence
And by the fact that we were lovers once,
By all the years of friendship we have seen,
By love itself, I charge you now Ramin

To read this letter to the very end,
So you may know the fortunes of your friend . . .

. . . You say you've sworn that you will never see
Your Vis again for all eternity,
But didn't you once swear to me that I
Would be your only love until you die?
Which of these oaths should I believe is true?
This one or that one then, which of the two?
Your vows veer like the wind, your oaths flow on
Like streams of water and are quickly gone –
Now wind and water are great things, but they
Can't stay in one place for a single day!
You're like a cloth shot through with silver thread,
It's one hue, then another hue instead;
Or like a gold coin journeying through the land
By constant passages from hand to hand.
Who have you known for love like me? If you
Won't stay with me, who will you stay with? Who?
Look at your evil deeds, all that you've done
Has meant our noble reputation's gone.
First, you seduced another's wife, the shame
Of this besmirched an honoured family's name;
Second, you swore an oath that you then broke
And spoke fair words, and lied too as you spoke;
Third, you betrayed your faithful lover who
Had never hurt or harmed or injured you;
Fourth, you insulted one who loves you more
Than all the world, and whom you still ignore.
I am still Vis, Vis of the sun-like face,
Whose tumbling hair still curls with musky grace,
I am still Vis, whose glance is like the spring,
Whose steadfast love will outlast everything,
I am still Vis, the moon when she is full,
I am still Vis, whose mouth's delectable,

I am still Vis, whom every beauty blesses,
I am still Vis, queen of all sorceresses,
When you were Solomon I was Bilqis,[4]
I am still Vis, I am still Vis, I'm Vis!
 I can find better lords than you, but you
Won't find my like, whatever you might do.
Whenever you reject me, you will learn
How harsh your Vis can be when you return;
Ramin, don't do this, you'll regret it, Vis
And Vis alone can make your sorrows cease;
Ramin, don't do this, Gol will soon disgust you,
But Vis will turn away then and not trust you;
Ramin, don't do this, you are drunk, that's why
You broke your oath to me with this new lie;
Ramin, don't do this, when sobriety
Returns you won't have either Gol or me –
Ah how you'll whine and grovel then before me,
Your faced pressed in the dust, how you'll implore me
To take you back again, but you will find
None of your pleas will alter Vis's mind.
You tired of my sweet lips, and I know you
Without a doubt will tire of Gol's lips too . . .
. . . But let this warn you, when all's said and done
You have your Rose now but your garden's gone,
You have the moon that shines for you at night,
But you have lost the sun's life-giving light;
You love your Judas tree, but can't you see
You lost your orchard when you gained this tree?
Have you forgotten all that bitterness,
That wild desire, that passionate distress?
If you but dreamt of me, Ramin, you thought
You were a king with all that kingship brought,
If you were dying and you caught my scent
Your health returned and every sickness went;

---

4. Bilqis: the Queen of Sheba and Solomon's lover.

But that's what thoughtless men are like, Ramin –
Their hearts forget the joys and griefs they've seen.
And then you sigh, 'I've lost my youth', and cry
'Alas for all my life that's now gone by.'
I lost my youth in loving you, I lost
My life in faithfulness, and at what cost!
You seemed so sweet, a sugar plant – I'd sow
My plant and nourish it and watch it grow,
And it would yield me sugar when it grew;
But bitterness is all I've seen from you!
When I consider all that I have done,
When I remember all I've undergone,
And all for you, fire rages in my brain,
I weep an Oxus for my pointless pain,
What hardships I've endured for you, Ramin –
And why? I've seen from you what I have seen!
You dug the pit, my nurse pushed me inside it,
Then sat herself down happily beside it;
You brought the wood, my nurse set fire to it –
And I was burnt just as my foes saw fit!
I don't know whether I should rail at you
Or her more; you're to blame, but she is too.

 But though I've seen your cruel unfaithfulness,
And felt your brand, and suffered such distress,
Though you have lit this fire within my blood,
And left me like a donkey stuck in mud,
Though you have made me weep without relief
So that I seem an Oxus formed from grief,
My heart still won't allow me to abuse you
Before God's throne; ah no, Vis can't accuse you!
Oh may it never happen that I see
Your suffering, since your suffering tortures me.
But now I'll write ten sections of this letter
So that, Ramin, you'll understand me better;
And, writing them, the very pen will run
With blood before this anguished letter's done.

301

Eventually Ramin returns to Vis, and the major plot difference between Vis and Ramin *and* Tristan and Isolde *is that* Vis and Ramin *ends happily with the lovers united in marriage. This becomes possible when Mobad is killed by a wild boar; Gorgani prefaces the incident by a meditation on fate, time, and death:*

> How well we think we know the world, although
> Its ligatures are things we never know.
> How well they're hidden, and how strong the Fate
> That keeps the world's transactions in this state!
> The world is sleep, we're dreams, and why should we
> Imagine this is where we'll always be?
> The world's conditions alter, and renew,
> And won't stay always as we wish them to.
> When love appears, the world can't tell apart
> Goodness and evil in the human heart,
> And it won't stay the friend of any lover
> Until his love's accomplished and is over;
> To trust the devious world with love's to tell
> A blind man to become your sentinel.
> Its various meretricious trinkets hide
> The truth, which stays unseeable inside,
> It's like a conjuring trick, and what we see
> Is not in fact how things turn out to be.
> It's like a caravanserai, which men
> Pass through, never to pass that way again;
> A moment's all that anyone can stay,
> No longer; then he too is on his way.
> It's like an archer who, year after year,
> Shoots endless arrow shafts that disappear
> Into the dark; he has no notion where,
> Or how, they strike, or drop down from the air.
> Or you would say it's like a crone whose face
> Has somehow kept its youth's bewitching grace,
> Who every moment thrusts into the grave
> Another husband who's become her slave.

We struggle for its wealth, with so much pain,
Till neither we nor any wealth remain;
We see an army, and we see a king,
Time passes by, and we see no such thing.
And in our day our generation thrives,
The group of men with whom we share our lives,
And this day passes by, it goes, and then
Another comes, and with it other men.
This is so strange to me now, and I find
It breeds black melancholy in my mind;
I don't know what time passing is, or what
Its tricks on us betoken in its plot –
That such a king as King Mobad, whose reign
Had brought the world such pleasure and such pain,
Should end his days so wretchedly! Alas
That all that he had hoped would come to pass
Should stay as figures in his heart and eyes
Which he perceived, but could not realize!

He pitched camp in Amol, and spent the night
In drinking wine, in pleasure and delight,
Giving his nobles robes, handing the poor
Money and weapons for the coming war:
Wine gave Mobad the happiness he sought,
Now see the hangover that morning brought.
The king was seated with his nobles when
A cry came from the tents that housed their men;
It happened that the camp was pitched beside
A place where various stream beds coincide,
And here a boar appeared, an animal
As violent and as uncontrollable
As is a maddened elephant; the boar
Was in the midst of men, behind, before,
All yelling at it, as it ran and found
The entrance to the royal camping ground.

The king came from his tent now to confront it,
And mounted his quick polo horse to hunt it;
The javelin that he held within his grasp
Had pitch black feathers fixed upon its hasp,
And it had shown a myriad foes the way
To death's black door, before that fateful day.
Now, like a raging lion, King Mobad
Hurled the black lance with all the strength he had;
It missed its mark, and with tumultuous force
The boar attacked the legs of Mobad's horse,
And got its tusks beneath the gut, and gored
The horse's belly as it reared and roared;
Rider and horse together now, pell-mell,
As though the moon and sky had fallen, fell.
The struggling king could not escape before
He was impaled there by the charging boar
Whose thrusting tusks now tore his flesh apart
Up from his navel to his beating heart,
Ripping the place where hate and love are housed;
The lamp of love, the blaze of hate, were doused.
The king of kings was dead, and darkness fell
Upon the noblemen who'd wished him well:
How easily this king, who had enjoyed
Such homage and such glory, was destroyed!

From *Faces of Love: Hafez and the Poets of Shiraz*
(2012, 2013)

Poems by Hafez

Hafez (c. 1315–c. 1389) is considered to be the major lyric poet of Persian literature. His poems are often strikingly ambiguous, and whether they are to be considered as primarily secular or primarily mystical has been a major point of scholarly contention; what is undeniable is that many of them can be read as either or both, and that this would seem to be deliberate. He was clearly a poet who did not wish his poems to be pinned down to one paraphrasable meaning.

    Ah God forbid that I relinquish wine
        when roses are in season;
    How could I do this when I'm someone who
        makes such a show of Reason?

    Where's a musician, so that I can give
        the profit I once found
    In self-control and knowledge for a flute's songs,
        and a lute's sweet sound?

    The endless arguments within the schools –
        whatever they might prove –
    Sickened my heart; I'll give a little time
        to wine now, and to love.

    Where is the shining messenger of dawn
        that I might now complain
    To my good fortune's harbinger of this
        long night of lonely pain?

But when did time keep faith with anyone?
        bring wine, and I'll recall
The tales of kings, of Jamshid and Kavus,
        and how time took them all.

I'm not afraid of sins recorded in
        my name — I'll roll away
A hundred such accounts, by His benevolence
        and grace, on Judgment Day.

This lent soul, that the Friend once gave into
        Hafez's care, I'll place
Within His hands again, on that day when
        I see Him face to face.

★

Where is the news we'll meet, that from
        this life to greet you there   I may arise?
I am a bird from paradise,
        and from this world's cruel snare   I will arise.

Now by my love for you, I swear
        that if you summon me
To be your slave, from all existence
        and its sovereignty   I will arise.

O Lord, make rain fall from your cloud
        sent to us as a guide,
Send it before, like scattered dust
        that's wind-blown far and wide,   I will arise.

Sit by my dust with wine and music:
        from my imprisonment
Beneath the ground, within my grave,
        dancing, drawn by your scent,   I will arise.

Rise now my love, display your stature,
    your sweetness, and I'll be,
Like Hafez, from the world itself
    and from my soul set free ...   I will arise.

And though I'm old, if you'll embrace
    my tightly in your arms all night
Then from your side, as dawn appears,
    young in the morning light,   I will arise.

★

My heart, good fortune is the only friend
    going along beside you that you need,
A breeze that's scented with Shiraz's gardens
    is all the guard to guide you that you need.

Poor wretch, don't leave your lover's home again,
    don't be in such a hurry to depart –
A corner of our Sufi meeting-place,
    the journey in your heart ... are all you need.

The claims of home, the promises you made
    an ancient friend – these are enough to say
When making your excuses to the travellers
    who've been along life's way ... they're all you need.

If grief should leap out from some corner of
    your stubborn heart and ambush you, confide
Your troubles to our ancient Zoroastrian –
    his precincts will provide ... you all you need.

Sit yourself down upon the wine-shop's bench
    and take a glass of wine – this is your share
Of all the wealth and glory of the world,
    and what you're given there ... is all you need.

Let go, and make life easy for yourself,
>   don't strain and struggle, always wanting more;
A glass of wine, a lover lovely as
>   the moon — you may be sure . . . they're all you need.

The heavens give the ignorant their head,
>   desire's the only bridle they acknowledge —
Your fault is that you're clever and accomplished,
>   and this same sin of knowledge . . . is all you need.

And you require no other prayer, Hafez,
>   than that prayed in the middle of the night;
This and the morning lesson you repeat
>   as dawn displays her light . . . are all you need.

Don't look for gifts from others; in both worlds —
>   this world, the world that is to come — your king's
Kind bounty, and the Lord's approval, are
>   the two essential things . . . they're all you need.

★

Mild breeze of morning, gently tell
>   that errant, elegant gazelle
She's made me wander far and wide
>   about the hills and countryside.

My sugar-lipped, sweet girl — oh may
>   you live forever and a day! —
Where is your kindness? Come now, show it
>   to your sweet-talking parrot-poet.

My rose, does vanity restrain you?
>   does beauty's arrogance detain you
From seeking out this nightingale
>   who wildly sings, to no avail?

With gentleness and kindness lies
        the surest way to win the wise,
Since birds that have become aware
        of ropes and traps are hard to snare.

When you sit safely with your love
        sipping your wine, be mindful of
Those struggling lovers who still stray,
        wind-tossed upon their weary way.

I don't know why she isn't here,
        why her tall presence won't appear,
Or why the full moon of her face,
        and her black eyes, avoid this place.

No fault can be imputed to
        your beauty's excellence, or you,
Except that there is not a trace
        of truth or kindness in your face.

When Hafez speaks, it's no surprise
        if Venus dances in the skies
And leads across the heavens' expanse
        Lord Jesus in the whirling dance.

★

With wine beside a gently flowing brook – this is best;
Withdrawn from sorrow in some quiet nook – this is best;
Our life is like a flower's that blooms for ten short days,
Bright laughing lips, a friendly fresh-faced look – this is best.

★

My friend, hold back your heart from enemies,
Drink shining wine with handsome friends like these;
With art's initiates undo your collar –
Stay buttoned up with ignoramuses.

★

To give up wine, and human beauty? and to give up love?
                                  No, I won't do it.
A hundred times I said I would; what was I thinking of?
                                  No, I won't do it.

To say that paradise, its houris, and its shade are more
To me than is the dusty street before my lover's door?
                                  No, I won't do it.

Sermons, and wise men's words, are signs, and that's how we should
   treat them;
I mouthed such metaphors before, but now – I won't repeat them;
                                  No, I won't do it.

I'll never understand myself, I'll never really know me,
Until I'm with the wine-shop's clientele, and that will show me;
                                  I have to do it.

The preacher told me, 'Don't drink wine', contempt was in the
   saying;
And I said, 'Sure.' Why should I listen to these donkeys braying?
                                  No, I won't do it.

The sheikh was angry when he told me, 'Give up love!' My brother,
There's no point in our arguing about it, so why bother?
                                  And I won't do it.

My abstinence is this: that when I wink and smile at beauty
It won't be from the pulpit in the mosque – I know my duty;
                              No, I won't do it.

Hafez, good fortune's with the Magian sage, and I am sure
I'll never cease to kiss the dust that lies before his door;
                              No, I won't do it.

★

A flower, without a friend's face there, I think
                              that isn't good
And spring time, if there isn't wine to drink,
                              that isn't good

A stroll through gardens, or a wooded place,
Without a pretty tulip-blushing face
                              that isn't good

A cypress swaying, and a rose unfolding,
Without a nightingale's melodious scolding
                              that isn't good

A sweet-lipped, sexy lover near, if this is
To be with no embraces and no kisses
                              that isn't good

Wine in a garden can be sweet, but when
We have no friend to talk and listen, then
                              that isn't good

And anything the mind dreams, in the end,
Unless it is the features of our friend,
                              that isn't good

The soul's a useless coin, Hafez — not worth
Your casting, as an offering, on the earth
                                that isn't good

★

Of all the roses in the world
        a rosy face . . . is quite enough for me;
Beneath this swaying cypress tree
        a shady place . . . is quite enough for me.

May hypocrites find somewhere else
        to cant and prate —
Of all this weighty world, a full
        wine-glass's weight . . . is quite enough for me.

They hand out heaven for good deeds!
        the monastery
Where Magians live is better for
        a sot like me . . . that's quite enough for me.

Sit by this stream and watch as life
        flows swiftly on —
This emblem of the world that's all
        too quickly gone . . . is quite enough for me.

See how the world's bazaar pays cash,
        see the world's pain —
And if you're not content with this
        world's loss and gain . . . they're quite enough for me.

My friend is here with me — what more
        should I desire?
The riches of our talk are all
        that I require . . . they're quite enough for me.

Don't send me from your door, O God,
    to paradise –
For me, to wait here at your street's
    end will suffice . . . that's quite enough for me.

Hafez, don't rail against your fate!
    your nature flows,
As does your verse, like water as
    it comes and goes . . . that's quite enough for me.

*

Dear friends, that friend with whom we once
    caroused at night –
His willing services to us
    and our delight . . . remember this.

And in your joy, when tinkling bells
    and harps are there,
Include within your songs the sound
    of love's despair . . . remember this.

When wine bestows a smile upon
    your server's face,
Keep in your songs, for lovers then,
    a special place . . . remember this.

So all that you have hoped for is
    fulfilled at last?
All that we talked of long ago,
    deep in the past . . . remember this.

When love is faithful, and it seems
    nothing can hurt you,
Know that the world is faithless still
    and will desert you . . . remember this.

If Fortune's horse bolts under you
            then call to mind
Your riding whip, and see your friends
            aren't left behind . . . remember this.

O you, who dwell in splendour now,
            glorious and proud,
Pity Hafez, your threshold's where
            his face is bowed . . . remember this.

★

May I remember always when
            your glance in secrecy met mine,
And in my face your love was like
            a visibly reflected sign.

May I remember always when
            your chiding eyes were like my death
And your sweet lips restored my life
            like Jesus's reviving breath.

May I remember always when
            we drank our wine as darkness died,
My friend and I, alone at dawn,
            though God was there too, at our side.

May I remember always when
            your face was pleasure's flame, and my
Poor fluttering heart was like a moth
            that's singed and is about to die.

May I remember always when
            the company that we were in
Was so polite, and when it seemed
            only the wine would wink and grin!

May I remember always when
        our goblet laughed with crimson wine –
What tales passed back and forth between
        your ruby lips, my dear, and mine!

May I remember always when
        I was a canopy unfurled
That shaded you, and you were like
        the new moon riding through the world.

May I remember always when
        I sat and drank in wine-shops where
What I can't find in mosques today
        accompanied the drinkers there.

May I remember always when
        the jewels of verse Hafez selected
Were set out properly by you,
        arranged in order, and corrected.

            ★

What memories! I once lived on
        the street that you lived on,
And to my eyes how bright the dust
        before your doorway shone!

We were a lily and a rose,
        our talk was then so pure
That what was hidden in your heart
        and what I said were one!

And when our hearts discoursed
        with wisdom's ancient words
Love's commentary solved each crux
        within our lexicon.

I told my heart that I would never be
    without my friend;
But when our efforts fail, and hearts
    are weak, what can be done?

Last night, for old time's sake, I saw
    the place where we once drank;
A cask was lying there, its lees
    like blood; mud was its bung.

How much I wandered, asking why
    the pain of parting came –
But Reason was a useless judge,
    and answers? He had none.

And though it's true the turquoise seal
    of Bu Es'haq shone brightly,
His splendid kingdom and his reign
    were all too quickly gone.

Hafez, you've seen a strutting partridge
    whose cry sounds like a laugh –
He's careless of the hawk's sharp claws
    by which he'll be undone.

★

For years my heart inquired of me
    where Jamshid's sacred cup might be,
And what was in its own possession
    it asked from strangers, constantly;
Begging the pearl that's slipped its shell
    from lost souls wandering by the sea.

Last night I took my troubles to
        the Magian sage whose keen eyes see
A hundred answers in the wine;
        laughing, he showed the cup to me –
I asked him, 'When was this cup
        that shows the world's reality

Handed to you?' He said, 'The day
        Heaven's vault of lapis lazuli
Was raised, and marvellous things took place
        by Intellect's divine decree,
And Moses' miracles were made
        and Sameri's apostasy.'

He added then, 'That friend they hanged
        high on the looming gallows tree –
His sin was that he spoke of things
        which should be pondered secretly,
The page of truth his heart enclosed
        was annotated publicly.

But if the Holy Ghost once more
        should lend his aid to us we'd see
Others perform what Jesus did –
        since in his heartsick anguish he
Was unaware that God was there
        and called His name out ceaselessly.'

I asked him next, 'And beauties' curls
        that tumble down so sinuously,
What is their meaning? Whence do they come?'
        'Hafez,' the sage replied to me,
'Their source is your distracted heart
        that asks these questions constantly.'

★

I see no love in anyone,
Where, then, have all the lovers gone?
And when did all our friendship end,
And what's become of every friend?

Life's water's muddied now, and where
Is Khezr[1] to guide us from despair?
The rose has lost its colouring,
What's happened to the breeze of spring?

A hundred thousand flowers appear
But no birds sing for them to hear –
Thousands of nightingales are dumb,
Where are they now? Why don't they come?

For years no rubies have been found
In stony mines deep underground;
When will the sun shine forth again?
Where are the clouds brim-full of rain?

Who thinks of drinking now? No one.
Where have the roistering drinkers gone?
This was a town of lovers once,
Of kindness and benevolence,

And when did kindness end? What brought
The sweetness of our town to naught?
The ball of generosity
Lies on the field for all to see –

---

4. Khezr: the keeper of the waters of eternal life.

No rider comes to strike it; where
Is everyone who should be there?
Silence, Hafez, since no one knows
The secret ways that heaven goes;

Who is it that you're asking how
The heavens are revolving now?

Poems by Jahan Khatun

Princess Jahan Malek Khatun (c. 1325–c. 1390) was the niece of Hafez's chief patron, King Abu Es'haq who ruled Shiraz from 1343 to 1353. A number of her poems allude to poems by Hafez (one quotes a poem of his verbatim), and it is virtually certain that Hafez and Jahan Khatun knew one another. All the men in her family were killed when the warlord Mobarez al-Din took over the rule of Shiraz in 1353, and it seems she was lucky to escape with her life. Most of her poems are love poems, but a few comment on the political struggles she lived through.

I swore I'd never look at him again,
I'd be a Sufi, deaf to sin's temptations;
I saw my nature wouldn't stand for it –
From now on I renounce renunciations.

★

Last night, my love, my life, you lay with me,
I grasped your pretty chin, I fondled it,
And then I bit, and bit, your sweet lips till
I woke ... It was my fingertip I bit.

★

My love's an ache no ointments can allay now;
My soul's on fire – how long you've been away now!
I said, 'I will be patient while he's gone.'
(But that's impossible ... it's one whole day now ...)

★

My heart, sit down, welcome love's pain,
    and make the best of it:

The rose is gone, the thorns remain,
    so make the best of it.
My heart said, 'No! I can't endure
    this sadness any longer . . .'
I said, 'You've no choice, don't complain,
    just make the best of it.'

★

Always, whatever else you do, my heart
Try to be kind, try to be true, my heart:
And if he's faithless, all may yet be well —
Who knows what he might do? Not you, my heart.

★

Shiraz when spring is here — what pleasure equals this?
With streams to sit by, wine to drink, and lips to kiss,
With mingled sounds of drums and lutes and harps and flutes;
Then, with a nice young lover near, Shiraz is bliss.

★

I know you think that there are other friends for me than you:
    Not so.
And that apart from loving you I've other things to do:
    Not so.

Belovèd, out of pity, take my hand before I fall,
You think the world can give me other loves to cling on to?
    Not so.

You strike me like a harp, play on me like a flute — and now
You have the nerve to claim that I have had enough of you?
    Not so.

What heavy sorrows weigh me down, and crush my abject
    soul!
Can anything be harder than your absence to live through?
        Not so.

Your eyes are languorous and rob my wakeful eyes of sleep,
Are any curls as wild as yours, as lovely and untrue?
        Not so.

You say my heart has not been hurt by your disdain. It has.
Has any lover suffered love's despair as I do now for you?
        Not so.

You have so many slaves, all finer than I am, I know –
But can you point to one more wretched in your retinue?
        Not so.

                    ★

Come here a moment, sit with me, don't sleep tonight,
Consider well my heart's unhappy plight, tonight;

And let your face's presence lighten me, and give
The loveliness of moonlight to the night, tonight.

Be kind now to this stranger, and don't imitate
Life as it leaves me in its headlong flight, tonight.

Be sweet to me now as your eyes are sweet, don't twist
Away now like your curls, to left and right, tonight;

Don't sweep me from you like the dust before your door;
Dowse all the flames of longing you ignite, tonight.

Why do you treat me with such cruelty now, my friend,
So that my tears obliterate my sight, tonight?

If, for a moment, I could see you in my dreams
I'd know the sum of all this world's delight, tonight.

⋆

Here, in the corner of a ruined school,
(More ruined even than my heart), I wait

While men declare that there's no goodness in me.
I sit alone, and brood upon my fate,

And hear their words, like salt rubbed in my wounds,
And tell myself I must accept my state:

I don't want wealth, and I don't envy them
The ostentatious splendour of the great.

What do they want from me though, since I've nothing?
Now that I'm destitute, and desolate?

⋆

For most of these long nights I stay awake
And go to bed as dawn begins to break;
I think that eyes that haven't seen their friend
Might get some sleep then . . . this is a mistake.

⋆

How long will heaven's heartless tyranny
Which keeps both rich and poor in agony

Go on? The dreadful happenings of these times
Have torn up by the roots Hope's noble tree,

And in the garden of the world you'd say
They've stripped the leaves as far as one can see.

That cypress which was once the cynosure
Of souls, they've toppled ignominiously;

I cry to heaven above, again I cry,
How long will this injustice fall on me?

What can I tell my grieving heart, that won't
Let dearest friends assuage its misery?

You'd say heaven's stuffed its ears with scraps of cotton
Simply to show that it's ignoring me!

∗

Most people in the world want power and money,
And just these two; that's all they're looking for.
They're faithless, callous, and unkind – the times
Are filled with squabbles, insurrections, war,
And everyone puts caution first, since now
Few friends exist of whom one can be sure.

Men flee from one another like scared deer,
And for a bit of bread the rabble roar
As though they'd tear each other's guts apart.
And why are men determined to ignore
The turning of the heavens, which must mean
The world will change, as it has done before?

But in their souls they are Your slaves, and search
The meadows for the cypress they adore;
My heart's an untamed doe, who haunts Your hills,
And whom no noose has ever snared before.

*

On the death of her infant daughter

O God, I beg you, open wide
    the gates of heaven
For one to whom a heavenly nature
    had been given;

Grant her a place in paradise,
    and may the throngs
Of lovely angels welcome her
    where she belongs;

Keep far from her this world's desires,
    its grief and spite;
Bestow your grace on her, and fill
    her soul with light.

*

My friend, who was so kind and faithful once,
Has changed his mind now, and I don't know why;

I think it must be in my wretched stars –
He feels no pity for me when I cry.

Oh I complain of your cruel absence, but
Your coming here's like dawn's breeze in the sky;

That oath you swore to and then broke – thank God
It's you who swore, and is foresworn, not I!

I didn't snatch one jot of joy before
You snatched your clothes from me and said goodbye;

I didn't thank you, since I wasn't sure
You'd really been with me, or just passed by.

How envious our clothes were when we lay
Without them, clasped together, you and I!

Your curls have chained my heart up; this is right —
Madmen are chained up, as they rage and sigh.

They say the world's lord cherishes his slaves;
So why's he harsh to me? I don't know why.

*

Heart, in his beauty's garden, I —
    like nightingales — complain,
And of his roses now for me
    only the thorns remain;

My friends have gathered flowers, but I,
    because of all his harshness,
Can find no flowers to gather here
    and search for them in vain.

My heart is filled with suffering;
    and all my doctor says is,
'Sugar from him, and nothing else,
    will lessen your heart's pain.'

I've filled the world with love for him,
    so why do I receive
Such cruelty from my dearest love,
    again, and yet again?

My free-will's gone from me, so how
      can my poor ears accept
All the advice my clever tutor's
      homilies contain?

No, in the pre-dawn darkness, I
      am like the nightingale
That in the orchards sings the rose
      its old love-sick refrain.

I hear it's strangers whom you welcome,
      whom you make much of now;
Let me then be a stranger in
      the kingdom where you reign.

*

I didn't know my value then, when I
      was young, so long ago;
And now that I have played my part out here,
      what is it that I know?

I know that, now that both of them have gone,
      life's good and bad passed by
As quickly in my youth as dawn's first breeze
      forsakes the morning sky.

How many ardent birds of longing then
      were lured down from the air
By my two ringlets' curls and coils, to be
      held trapped and helpless there!

And in youth's lovely orchard then I raised
      my head as prettily,
As gracefully, above the greensward there,
      as any cypress tree;

Until, with charming partners to oppose me,
    I took up lovers' chess,
And lost so many of love's pieces to
    my partners' handsomeness –

And then how often on the spacious field
    of beauty I urged on
My hopeful heart's untiring steed, always
    pursuing what was gone.

Now, as no shoots or leaves remain to me
    from youth, and youth's delight,
I fit myself in my old age to face
    the darkness of the night.

★

I am still drunk that you were here,
    and you were mine,
And once again I stretch my hand out
    for that wine;

As your drunk eyes could not bestir
    themselves, I too
Can't move; as you love wine, I love
    the wine that's you.

And I will ask the gentle morning
    breeze to bear
A message to my love who has
    such musky hair,

Since that black hair's sweet scent, from being
    next to me,
Has made me like a musk deer come
    from Tartary.

I fainted when you were not here,
        I could not stand –
Be with me now my love, support me,
        grasp my hand;

Oh I was so distracted, heart-sick,
        that I gave
My soul into your ringlets' snare,
        I was your slave;

My eyes wept tears of blood while you
        were never there,
My feet were shackled in your curls'
        enclosing snare.

How sad my heart was then! But, God
        be praised, relief
Has now arrived for me; I have
        escaped from grief!

★

Your face usurps the fiery glow and hue
        of roses;
And with your face here, what have I to do
        with roses?

Your ringlets' fragrance is so sweet, my friend,
No fragrant rose-scent could entice me to
        seek roses –

Besides, the faithless roses' scent will fade,
Which is a serious drawback, in my view,
        of roses;

And if the waters of eternal life
Had touched their roots, so that they bloomed anew,
    these roses,

When could they ever form a bud as sweet
As your small mouth, which is more trim and true
    than roses?

★

A happy heart's the place for plans and piety,
And wealth's a fine foundation for sobriety:
A weak and wasted arm can't wield a warrior's sword,
A broken heart can't act with cold propriety.

★

From now on I have sworn
    I won't let dreams deceive me,
Since pointless dreams have made
    my spirit almost leave me;

My poor heart dreamt of you
    so earnestly it seems
Your image turned my flesh
    into the stuff of dreams.

I gave my head, heart, soul
    and faith to you – so who
Informed you killing me's
    a legal thing to do?

Have mercy on me now,
    pity my wretchedness,
I've reached the limits of
    exhaustion and distress.

Now by his doe-like eyes,
        the full moon of his face,
His eyebrow's arch that's like
        the new moon in its grace,

By his bright cheeks, the rose
        and jasmine mingled there,
By his moist lips, and by
        the sweet scent of his hair,

By my parched, thirsty lips,
        by meeting him at night,
By his proud stride, and by
        his sapling-slender height,

I swear that in this night
        of his long absence, my
Poor face is pallid as
        the pale moon in the sky;

I swear that I despair
        of heart and soul, and of
Both this world and the next,
        without him, and his love.

'You're like the nightingale'
        he said, 'whose lovesick woe
Harangues the rose! Poor wretch,
        stop whining now, and go!'

        ★

At dawn my heart said I should go
        into the garden where
I'd pick fresh flowers, and hope to see
        his flower-like beauty there.

I took his hand in mine, and oh
    how happily we strayed
Among the tulip beds, and through
    each pretty grassy glade;

How sweet the tightness of his curls
    seemed then, and it was bliss
To grasp his fingers just as tight,
    and snatch a stealthy kiss.

For me to be alone beside
    that slender cypress tree
Cancels the thousand injuries
    he's meted out to me

He's a narcissus, tall and straight!
    and so how sweet to bow
My head like violets at his feet
    and kiss the earth there now.

But your drunk eyes don't deign to see me,
    although I really think
It's easy to see someone who's
    the worse for love or drink.

And though it's good to weep beneath
    God's cloud of clement rain,
It's also good to laugh like flowers
    when sunlight shines again.

My heart was hurt by his 'check-mate';
    I think I must prepare
To seek out wider pastures then,
    and wander off elsewhere.

Jahan, be careful not to say
    too much; it's pitiful
To give a jewel to someone who
    can't see it's valuable.

★

How sweet those days when we were still
    together; when we cared
For one another, and our grief
    and happiness were shared!

We used no waspish tongues to wound
    each other's hearts; we swore
That we'd be one another's shields,
    faithful for evermore!

And would, thanks be to God, be famed
    for how much we'd dispense
In charity, and for our buildings'
    bold magnificence.

For years we took our pleasure, laughed
    aloud – it was as though
We were spring flowers, and happiness
    was all that we could know;

And we were kind, considerate,
    politely intimate –
As gentle as the morning breeze
    with every soul we met.

We spread our light throughout the world
    as if we were the sun,
And like the sun itself we dried
    dew's tears for everyone.

★

His glances trap my heart within their snare,
And straightaway his glances stray elsewhere;

He is the brightness of my eyes, so why should he
Be lighting others' eyes up over there?

I've loved him faithfully for years; but he's
Habitually unfaithful everywhere.

In all the world, no heart is safe from him,
There's not a single heart he'd care to spare!

My Fortune led me to Delusion's Garden,
And all that scoundrel said was, 'I don't care.'

The day we met I gave my soul to him.
And why? To have him leave me in despair?

The heart's the body's queen; and look, my love,
At your street's end – a queen stands begging there.

★

The roses have all gone; 'Goodbye,' we say; we must;
And I shall leave the busy world one day; I must.
My little room, my books, my love, my sips of wine –
All that is dear to me – they'll pass away; they must.

Notes on the Poems

Seeing the World

THE CITY OF ORANGE TREES (p. 52)

In *An Introduction to History – The Muqaddimah*, Ibn Khaldun quotes and explains the proverb with which this poem opens. The meeting that ends the poem occurred outside the walls of Damascus in 1401.

SYNCRETIC AND SECTARIAN (p. 53)

Dara Shukoh, the eldest son of Shah Jahan, translated the *Upanishads* into Persian with the avowed intention of finding common ground between Islam and Hindu beliefs. In 1659 he was murdered by his younger brother, who later became the emperor Aurungzeb, the most fanatically zealous of all the Moghul emperors.

ZULEIKHA SPEAKS (p. 59)

Zuleikha is the woman known in the Bible as Potiphar's wife. In one interpretation of the story Zuleikha represents the human soul wedded to the world (Potiphar) but 'illicitly' in love with the beauty of God, represented by Joseph.

WITTGENSTEIN IN GALWAY (p. 65)

'(In 1947) . . . he left Cambridge and settled for a while in Ireland . . . in a seaside hut in Galway, where the fishermen remarked on his ability to tame birds.' – Anthony Kenny, *Wittgenstein*.

MAXIMILIAN KOLBE (p. 74)

In Auschwitz this Polish priest voluntarily took upon himself the death sentence passed on another prisoner.

The Covenant

TO HIS WIFE (p. 89)

The opening words of Ausonius's poem are 'Uxor vivamus . . .', the title of the previous poem.

Belonging

HAYDN AND HOKUSAI (p. 179)

The last two lines of the poem are a translation of an inscription in the Red Fort, Delhi, built by the Moghul Emperor Shah Jahan (reigned 1627–1658).

IRAN TWENTY YEARS AGO (p. 181)

Hafez (c. 1315–c. 1389) is perhaps the greatest of Persian lyric poets. Like his predecessor Sa'di, and his contemporary the female poet Jahan Khatun, he was a native of Shiraz; the poems of all three often praise the beauty of the town, and the sweetness of its life. Nayshapour was the home town of Omar Khayyam, and of the Sufi poet Farid uddin Attar.

DIDO (p. 185)

The epigraph is from Nahum Tate's libretto to Purcell's *Dido and Aeneas*.

WEST SOUTH WEST (p. 187)

This poem was commissioned by BBC Radio's celebration of Britain's National Poetry Day (October 5th) 2000. A number of poets were each assigned a point of the compass, on which they were asked to write a sonnet. The historical and geographical details of this poem will be familiar to British readers. The Solent is a channel about fifteen miles long between the south coast of England and the Isle of Wight. Admiral Lord Nelson destroyed the French fleet at the Battle of Trafalgar (1805): he was mortally wounded during the battle, partly because he insisted on wearing his conspicuous admiral's uniform while on deck. His flagship, *The Victory*, is now in dry dock in Portsmouth harbour, and as a boy I often went around it.

TERESIA SHERLEY (p. 188)

The 'thrice admirable and undaunted Lady Teresia, the faithful wife of Sir Robert Sherley' was the daughter of a Circassian at the court of Shah Abbas (reigned 1587–1629) of Persia. She seems to have been more or less a present from the Shah to Sir Robert, an English adventurer employed for many years at the Persian court. The marriage was apparently a very happy one, and Teresia accompanied her husband on his travels in Europe, where he acted as the Shah's (largely unsuccessful) roving ambassador. For a while they settled in Sussex, at Petworth House; a Van Dyck portrait of Teresia still hangs there.

Esfahan was the capital of Persia during the reign of Shah Abbas. He and his successors made it one of the most beautiful cities in the Middle East, filling it with gardens and splendid public buildings, a number of which still survive. The carpets of Esfahan (mentioned in 'Aubade') are some of the most sumptuous the country produces.

SECRETS (p. 194)

Rostam is the main hero of the Persian epic, *The Shahnameh*. He is killed by his brother Shaghad, who digs a pit lined with stakes, into which Rostam falls.

A SE STESSO (p. 196)

The phrase means 'To Himself'. It is the title of a poem by Leopardi, in the shadow of which my poem was written.

'LIVE HAPPILY' (p. 197)

The French epigraph was said by his Alpine guide of the young John Ruskin.

GUIDES FOR THE SOUL (p. 198)

Psychopomp: 'A conductor of souls to the place of the dead. In Greek a name applied to Charon; more commonly to Hermes, the Anubis of Egypt, and to Apollo' – OED.

JUST SO (p. 210)

Rudaki was a Persian poet of the 10th century AD. One of his most beguiling poems begins, 'The scent of the stream of Muliyan comes to me continually / The memory of the kindness of my friend comes to me continually'. This poem is said to have been written at the request of a disgruntled band of warriors as a way of persuading their commander to return home. The ploy was successful.

A Trick of Sunlight

CHÈVREFEUILLE (p. 214)

The title refers to the twelfth-century poem of the same name by Marie de France, which uses honeysuckle (chèvrefeuille) and hazel growing together as emblems of the love of Tristan and Isolde.

HÉRÉDIA (p. 217)

José Maria de Hérédia (1842–1905) was born in Cuba; he lived in Paris for most of his life, where he was a leading member of the Parnassian group of poets, so called for their adherence to classical models. Most of his poems are sonnets, which are marked by a scrupulous formal precision united to often extravagant and highly romantic subject matter, much of it drawn from either the Roman past or mythology.

THE MAN FROM PROVINS (p. 218)

This poem is drawn from an incident briefly recounted in the memoirs of the soldier Jean, sire de Joinville, who had accompanied Louis IX of France, known as Saint Louis, on his crusade to the Holy Land (1248–1254). The expedition ended in disaster when Louis's troops were besieged and then forced to surrender at Damietta in northern Egypt. They were eventually ransomed, and returned home. The man who questions the narrator of the poem, after the king has dismissed him, is Joinville himself.

The still largely medieval town of Provins lies southeast of Paris; from having been one of the most important cities in France it began to decline economically in the thirteenth century and never recovered.

THE OLD MODEL'S ADVICE TO THE NEW MODEL (p. 220)

This was written for inclusion in *Fashioned Pleasures*, a chapbook of sonnets, by different poets, using the rhyme words of Shakespeare's Sonnet XX.

WHAT I THINK (p. 223)

This poem was written in response to Wendy Cope's poem of the same name in her book *If I Don't Know* (Faber, 2001).

TURGENIEV AND FRIENDS (p. 229)

Turgeniev's mother beat him unmercifully when he was a child. The great love of his life was the French operatic mezzo-soprano Pauline Viardot, sister of the famous Malibran. The two girls had been taught to sing by their father, a notoriously violent teacher who beat his pupils, including his daughters, for even trivial mistakes.

CYTHÈRE (p. 235)

Although this was originally the French name for Cythera, the island near which Aphrodite was born in the sea, it was also used by some poets (e.g. Ronsard) for the goddess herself. It is this latter use which is invoked in my poem.

YOUNG SCHOLAR (p. 236)

Amor de lonh, 'love from afar', is the central concern of much lyrical medieval European poetry.

SMALL TALK (p. 240)

'Interpretation is the revenge of the intellect upon art'
The title is a remark by Susan Sontag.

DIS'S DEFENCE (p. 243)

Dis is the god of the underworld, Hades in Greek mythology. He captured Persephone, the daughter of Zeus, and took her down to his kingdom, where he made her his queen. She returns to the earth every year, and this marks the beginning of spring, but always returns to her consort in Hades for the winter months.

WILLIAM McGONAGALL WELCOMES THE INITIATIVE FOR A GREATER ROLE FOR FAITH-BASED EDUCATION (p. 244)

William McGonagall (1825–1902) has the dubious reputation of being 'the writer of the worst poetry in English'. His metre is all over the place, and he never saw a sentimental commonplace he didn't feel was an admirable subject for a poem.

GOING, GOING ... (p. 269)

Urquhart, the 17th-century translator of Rabelais, and Aretino, the 16th-century Italian satirist/pornographer, both died as a result of a fit of unstoppable laughter.

INDEX OF TITLES

This list does not include poems in the Translations section.

6 a.m. Thoughts, 113

A Se Stesso, 196
'A world dies...', 191
Abandoned Churchyards, 108
Acculturation, 241
Acedia, 113
Admonition for the Seventh Decade, 266
Afkham, 130
After the Angels, 148
Aftershocks, 153
Among Ruins, 26
Anchorite, 44
'And who is good?...', 114
Anglais Mort à Santa Barbara, 224
Annunciation, 81
Anthony 1946–1966, 152
Are We Going the Same Way?, 247
Arghavan, 138
Art History, 163
At the Reception, 208
Aubade, 195
Auction – Job Lot, 106
Author, Translator..., 240

Baucis and Philemon, 83
Before Sleep, 219
Bit of Paternity, A, 205
Brahms, 253
Business Man's Special, The, 209
Buyer's Market, 46
Byzantine Coin, 26

Campanilismo, 266
Can We?, 234

Casanova, 184
Chagrin, 232
Checking Out While Checking In, 209
Chèvrefeuille, 214
Childhood, 31
Childhood of a Spy, 101
Christmas Poem, A, 107
City of Orange Trees, The, 52
Climbing, 58
Comfort, 150
Couples, 164
Cythère, 235

Damnation à la Mode, 240
Darwinian, 261
Dawn, 59
Déjà Lu, 207
Departure of the Myths, The, 117
Desert Stop at Noon, 50
Desire, 203
Desire, 166
Desire, 69
Desire, 34
Diana and Actaeon, 28
Dido, 185
Dis's Defence, 243
Discipline, 137
Diver, The, 21
'Do you remember those few hours we spent', 226
Don Giovanni, 57
Don Giovanni at the Opera, 35
Dream, A, 260
Driving, 226

345

Driving Westward, 246
Duchy and Shinks, 186

Edgar, 221
Edward FitzGerald, 96
Emblems, 248
Entry, An, 66
Epic Scholar, The, 37
Epitaph, 74
Epitaph, 163
Et in Arcadia Ego, 209
Euro-trash, 268
Evening, 118
Exile, 110
Exiles, 94
Expulsion from Eden, The, 27

Fall, The, 258
False Light, 64
Families, 32
Farewell to the Mentors, 204
Farsighted, 236
Fatherhood, 135
Finding, 240
Fireflies, 174
Flight, 156
Flying Back, 227
For my mother-in-law, during her last illness, 259
Four Visitations, 83
Fräulein X, 77

Games, 199
Getting Away, 214
Getting There, 87
Given Back, After Illness, 147
Going Home, 154
Going, going..., 270
Gold, 157
Góngora, 183
Government in Exile, 58

Growing Up, 207
Guides for the Soul, 198

Happiness, 216
Haydn and Hokusai, 179
Hearing a Balkan Dance in England, 108
Hérédia, 217
Heresy, 129
Hibernation, 192
Household Gods, 119

'I lay down in the darkness of my soul', 238
Ibn Battuta, 116
Ikon Angel, 42
Imitatio, 239
In History, 183
In Praise of Auden, 169
In the Gallery, 78
In the Restaurant, 186
'Interpretation is the revenge of the intellect upon art', 240
Into Care, 150
Introduction, The, 263
Iran Twenty Years Ago, 181
Irony and Love, 36

Jacob I, 84
Jacob II, 85
Janet Lewis, Reading Her Poems, 125
Jealousy, 123
Jesus on the Water, 41
Jigsaw, The, 80
Just a Small One, as You Insist, 203
Just So, 210

Keeping a Diary, 268
Kipling's Kim, Thirty Years On, 205

346

Lady with a Theorbo, 133
Late, 174
Later, 267
Learning a Language, 137
Leaving the Fair, 271
Leonardo, 72
Letter to Omar, A, 91
Lighthouse, The, 251
Listening, 222
Littoral, 45
'Live all you can; it's a mistake not to', 239
'Live happily', 197
Living in the World, 45
Love, 67
Love in Another Language, 35

Made in Heaven, 129
Magic ('I can imagine someone knowing you'), 239
Magic ('The child steps carefully'), 127
Making a Meal of It, 128
Man from Provins, The, 218
Maple Tree, The, 262
Mariam Darbandi, 104
Marriage as a Problem of Universals, 56
Masters, 161
Maximilian Kolbe, 74
May, 154
Me, You, 54
Memories of Cochin, 53
Metaphor, 58
Middle Age, 165
Middle East 1950s, 115
Mind-Body Problem, A, 202
Mirak, 157
Missing Tale, The, 255

Mohsen: A Gardener in California, 138
Monorhyme for Miscegenation, A, 146
Monorhyme for the Shower, A, 178
My Daughter Sleeping, 105
Mycenaean Brooch, A, 24
Mystery Novel, A, 248

Names ('Inapprehensible, the world'), 46
Names ('In *Inghilterra* you imagine love'), 159
Narcissus' Grove, 44
Near Coltishall, 102
New at It, 206
New Development, 260
New Reader, 162
Night on the Long-Distance Coach, 51
Night Thoughts, 180
No Going Back, 193
North-West Passage, 38
Not-Waking, 239
Novice, The, 44

Off-Shore Current, 90
Old, 208
Old Couple, 165
Old Man Seated Before a Landscape, 33
Old Model's Advice to the New Model, The, 220
On a Painting by Guardi, 73
On a Remark of Karl Kraus, 237
On an Etching by J. S. Cotman, 100
On the Iranian Diaspora, 140
Opening the Pyramid, 65
Out of Time, 194

'Outside the snow . . .', 135
Overheard in Khajuraho, 209

Pasts, 232
Paying for It, 269
Perfect Ending, A, 68
Personal Sonnet, A, 252
Petrarchan Sonnet, A, 184
Phaedra and Hippolytus, 69
Philosopher and Metaphysics, 66
Phoenix, The, 242
Photograph of Two Brothers, A, 152
Photograph: Tehran, 1920s, A, 98
Political Asylum, 182
Portrait Painter, 78
Pragmatic Therapy, 151
Preferences, 238

Qasideh for Edgar Bowers on his Seventieth Birthday, A, 167
Qatran, 134

Ransom, The, 103
Reading, 105
Reading After Opium, 45
Reason in his Kingdom, 33
Reconnoitring, 270
Recording of Giuseppe de Luca (1903), A, 64
Rembrandt Dying, 70
Rembrandt's *Return of the Prodigal Son*, 70
Repentance, 166
Richard Davis, 99

Sasanian Palace, A, 155
Saving Grace, The, 270
Scavenging After a Battle, 25
Sceptic, The, 225
Scholar as a Naughty Boy, The, 224

Secrets, 194
Semele, 83
Sentimental Misanthrope, The, 128
Service, 34
Shadows, 177
Shopping, 231
Shore, The, 22
Short History of Chess, A, 90
Simeon, 61
Small Talk, 208, 239
Socrates' Daimon, 134
Socratic Traveller, The, 43
Soteriological, 240
Spleen, 241
St Christopher, 62
St Eustace, 86
St George and the Villagers, 30
Still, 149
Storm in the Mid-West, A, 251
Student Reading *Vis and Ramin*, A, 272
Suicide, The, 153
Suzanne Doyle's Poems, 171
'Sweet Pleasure . . .', 192
Syncretic and Sectarian, 53

Tease, A, 166
Tenured in the Humanities, 161
Teresia Sherley, 188
'The heart has its abandoned mines . . .', 213
There, 241
'They are not long, the days of wine and roses . . .', 230
Three Emilys, 228
Three Versions of the Maker, 136
To 'Eshqi, 143
To Exorcize Regret, 68
To His Wife, 89
To Take Courage in Childhood, 253

To the Muse, 126
To the Persian Poets, 182
To Vis, 272
Touchwood, 151
Touring a Past, 23
Translating a Medieval Poem, 255
Translating Hafez, 109
Translating Hafez, or Trying To, 273
Translator's Nightmare, A, 172
Travelling ('Wild lavender and mint'), 49
Travelling ('You live for landscapes scudding past'), 89
Tribe of Ben, The, 97
Turgeniev and Friends, 229
Two East Anglian Poems, 96
Two Epigrams on Victory, 67

Under $6 a Bottle, 229
Undine, 114
'Uxor vivamus . . .', 87

'Vague, vagrant lives . . .', 57
Victorian, 200
Virgin Mary, The, 29
Visit to Grandmother's, A, 233

Walking the Dog, 257
Water, 216
We Should Be So Lucky, 160
West South West, 187
What, 191
What I Think, 223
What the Mind Wants, 79
Wil Mills (1969–2011), 256
William McGonagall Welcomes the Initiative for a Greater Role for Faith-Based Education, 244
William Morris, 245
Wine, 265

Winter, 62
Winter's Tale, A, 254
Wisdom, 123
With John Constable, 96
With Johnson's *Lives of the Poets*, 124
Withernsea, 63
Wittgenstein in Galway, 65
Woman on a Beach, 95
Words, 274
WWHD?, 274

Young Scholar, 236
Your Children Growing, 149
Youth of Telemachus, 31

Zuleikha Speaks, 59